D0881332

*Deliverance
from the Little Big Horn*

Deliverance from the Little Big Horn

*Doctor Henry Porter
and Custer's Seventh Cavalry*

Joan Nabseth Stevenson

UNIVERSITY OF OKLAHOMA PRESS : NORMAN

Library of Congress Cataloging-in-Publication Data

Stevenson, Joan Nabseth.
Deliverance from the Little Big Horn: Doctor Henry Porter and Custer's Seventh
Cavalry / Joan Nabseth Stevenson.
   p.   cm.
Includes bibliographical references and index.
ISBN 978-0-8061-4266-1 (hardcover : alk. paper)
1. Porter, Henry R., 1848–1903.
2. Little Bighorn, Battle of the, Mont., 1876
3. Surgeons—United States—Biography.
4. United States. Army. Cavalry, 7th—Biography.
I. Title.
E83.876.S76 2012
610.92—dc23
[B]

                                         2011045267

The paper in this book meets the guidelines for permanence and durability of the
Committee on Production Guidelines for Book Longevity of the Council on Library
Resources, Inc. ∞

1 2 3 4 5 6 7 8 9 10

For my father, Donald C. Nabseth
Native of North Dakota,
Boston surgeon,
And one who knows something
about stamina and a steady hand.

There is an old saw in the army that teaches that you can never know a man until having made a scout with him in bad weather.

Lieutenant John G. Bourke,
aide-de-camp to Brigadier General George Crook

Contents

Illustrations

———

Preface

WHEN LIEUTENANT COLONEL George Armstrong Custer and the men of his Seventh Cavalry approached the valley of the Little Big Horn River on June 25, 1876, they were accompanied by three surgeons. Doctor George Lord would continue on with Custer and ultimately ride to his death. The other two surgeons were assigned to Major Marcus Reno's battalion, which initiated the fighting at the southern end of the Indian village. When a vast force of warriors, well armed with repeating rifles, turned Reno's flank and threatened to encircle his entire command, the major ordered a charge to the top of a bluff about a mile away, seeking relative safety in elevation. While scaling the bluff, Doctor James DeWolf was shot seven times and killed. That left only the youngest and most robust of the three surgeons, twenty-eight-year-old Henry Renaldo Porter, who managed to ride through a gauntlet of Indians and up the steep bluffs to the hilltop position. There Doctor Porter assumed the medical care of the more than 350 men under Reno's command as they fought for their lives against as many as 2,000 Indian warriors menacing them from all sides.

Twelve hours later, after another fierce daylong fight on the twenty-sixth, the Indian village—nearly 7,000 people—broke camp to move south and closer to the Big Horn Mountains. They were done fighting. Reno's command took advantage of the unexpected reprieve to recover from the toll exacted by nearly sixteen hours of relentless attack. What the major and his men did not know at the time was that the cavalrymen led by Custer had ridden headlong into a contest with a superior

Indian force that quickly annihilated the battalion. The following day a column of soldiers under Brigadier General Alfred H. Terry and Colonel John Gibbon came to the rescue of those who remained on the hilltop.

Although Reno's two-day battle with the Indians had ended, Henry Porter's lifesaving medical work was only beginning as he attended to the wounds of sixty-eight soldiers and two Indian scouts and performed surgeries, including two amputations. Transported on mule or hand litters, the wounded endured a hazardous nighttime evacuation of fifteen miles, involving two river crossings, the scaling of a steep bluff, and a treacherous descent from the plateau to the safety of the steamboat *Far West*, waiting at the mouth of the Little Big Horn. Porter and his patients then endured a harrowing seven-hundred-mile journey by boat down the Yellowstone and Missouri Rivers until they reached the post hospital at Fort Abraham Lincoln, just below Bismarck, Dakota Territory, a passage undertaken at an unprecedented speed and completed in a mere fifty-four hours.

Deliverance from the Little Big Horn provides an original account of these extraordinary events. It places the Battle of the Little Big Horn in the context of the Seventh Cavalry's summer-long "Expedition against hostile Sioux," a campaign intended to coerce roaming bands of Sioux and Northern Cheyenne Indians onto the Great Sioux Reservation. Acting Assistant Surgeon Porter's personal story and unique medical perspective on this legendary episode serve as the basis for a compelling narrative history that looks beneath familiar historical events to recount the desperate struggle for survival, both from wounds inflicted by conventional weapons as well as from debilitations inevitably resulting from campaigning and fighting in the West: dehydration, hemorrhage, infection, and dietary and "filth" diseases. The medical dimension of the story—not least the grim conditions in Porter's hilltop field hospital and the ways in which the army managed to avoid leaving its wounded behind—offers a fresh perspective on the Little Big Horn. This drama is told against the background of the post–Civil War state of American medical science, which is revealed as stubbornly parochial in its resistance to the progressive germ theory of disease already being embraced in England and continental Europe, thanks to the research of Louis Pasteur, Joseph Lister, and Robert Koch. As a consequence, in America hands that aimed to cure also continued to infect. This larger medical context opens a window onto the gritty undercurrents of endurance and survival that—even more than the "hostile" Indians, it turns out—threatened the entire military effort in the summer of 1876.

As a civilian surgeon, Henry Porter served the army under a "contract." He performed his duties without the incentives of rank, promotion, or pension as he "bore the burden and heat of the day" like the regular soldiers under his care. The army often rewarded contract surgeons with brief written commendations, but these rarely atoned for the frequent slights and humiliations and the sheer indifference these professionals often experienced as noncommissioned participants. Twenty-two years after the Little Big Horn, in 1898, Porter was nominated for the Medal of Honor in recognition of his painstaking efforts to save the lives of more than fifty soldiers wounded in one of this country's most searing and controversial battles. Nothing came of the proposal. To this day the U.S. government has yet to recognize Porter for his outstanding feat of medical service.

I first encountered the material that forms the basis for this work when my father, Doctor Donald C. Nabseth, delivered the presidential address at the Boston Surgical Society in 1985, in which he recounted for his fellow physicians the story of the three surgeons at the Battle of the Little Big Horn. No doubt many in that audience identified with Harvard Medical School graduate James DeWolf, but my father was drawn to the quietly heroic figure of Henry Porter. A native of North Dakota, my father was born near the city of Bismarck, where Porter eventually settled. The affinity of the twentieth-century surgeon for his nineteenth-century predecessor ran deep. After hearing my father's talk, I realized that here was a slice of the story of Custer and the fight at the Little Big Horn that had yet to be told.

Deliverance
from the Little Big Horn

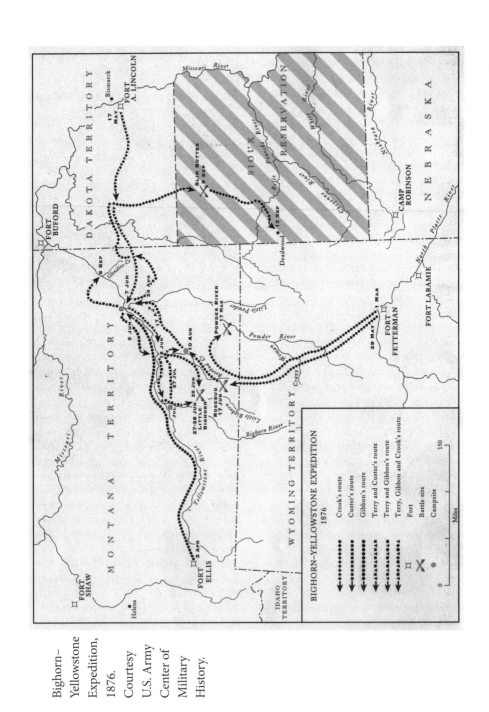

Bighorn–Yellowstone Expedition, 1876. Courtesy U.S. Army Center of Military History.

Witness

IN THE DEAD OF WINTER, January 1879, the military court of inquiry investigating the conduct of Major Marcus A. Reno convened in a public room in the elegant Palmer House Hotel in Chicago. Two and a half years had passed since the cry "Massacred" headlined the front page of nearly every major newspaper in the nation, challenging readers to make sense of the sudden annihilation of the famed "General" George Armstrong Custer and the 210 men in his command at the Battle of the Little Big Horn. The court had met to look into Reno's conduct during the battle and to address the damning criticism leveled at him by supporters of Custer, who claimed that Reno's cowardice and neglect of duty had cost Custer and his men their lives. The statute of limitations for a more serious court-martial had passed, but a sense of accountability could still be exacted.[1]

By 1879 the public disbelief of 1876 had evolved into curiosity, and the small room in the Palmer House quickly filled beyond capacity with reporters, gentlemen spectators, and even a few pairs of ladies, whose fashionable fur hats obstructed the view of those sitting in their vicinity. When Major Reno, a West Point graduate with the stockiness of his forty-five years, entered the room, necks craned as spectators sought to take in the man whose military reputation was now at stake. Straight dark hair combed back framed a full face, and a small mustache and the hint of a goatee below his lower lip indicated careful grooming. The steady gaze of the officer's dark eyes suggested self-possession. In the stiffened regalia of a full-dress uniform, Reno made a dramatic appearance in the courtroom, all the more so because he entered last.[2]

Sitting off to the side of the large tables occupied by the members of the court and Reno's defense team were twenty-three witnesses: eighteen military officers, also in full dress uniforms, and five civilians. Most had been members of the Seventh Cavalry on June 25, when it confronted a village of an estimated 7,000 Sioux and Northern Cheyenne encamped along the Greasy Grass, as the Indians called the Little Big Horn River. While the military officers among the witnesses largely had a common purpose—to rescue and preserve the reputation of the regiment from the tarnish of recklessness and disunity—the smaller civilian group shared no such sense of cohesion. Despite their less glamorous roles in the battle, the five civilians—two mule packers, one interpreter, one scout, and one surgeon—had also endured and survived the fights Reno led against overwhelming numbers of Indian warriors.[3]

One civilian in particular had worked without rest or relief for inhumanly long hours. Doctor Henry Porter had tended to the care of over fifty wounded soldiers corralled together in the heat and dust of a hastily made field hospital secured in the center depression of the hilltop position and surrounded by an unruly cordon of terrified cavalry horses and pack mules. Wound care and surgery had occupied Porter almost entirely during the fighting on June 25. Yet he had observed Reno's interactions with his officers before the start of the defensive battle, and this made him qualified to appear as a witness at the hearing.

On the tenth day of the inquiry, as a blue winter light filtered through the meeting room windows, Doctor Porter was summoned to the witness chair. His blond hair and handlebar mustache and his pale blue eyes testified to his mother's highland heritage, making an agreeable impression on reporters and spectators alike: they anticipated the forthright demeanor of a good Scot. In a dark wool frockcoat worn over a vest and a starched white shirt collar closed with a wide black ribbon bowtie, Porter appeared cosmopolitan, distinctly a cut above what most Chicagoans expected of a man from Bismarck, Dakota Territory. At age thirty-one and with his above-average height, Porter exuded good health and confidence. His testimony followed that of several military officers, and the courtroom seemed ready for a change in tone and message. Porter's evidence would carry weight.

Privately, the doctor felt ambivalent about Reno. The major had professed concern for the wounded soldiers, Porter could testify, and had refused to abandon them after gunfire was heard in the distance, even though other officers frantically urged him to hasten the entire command toward the sound, assuming that Custer was engaged in battle. But Porter also suspected that Reno's composure had been badly shaken earlier in a gruesome split-second event, when a well-placed shot to the head of Custer's favorite Indian scout, Bloody Knife, had splattered brains onto the major's face and uniform. In fact, his leadership and judgment would wane later in the day, forcing other officers to assume control.

Just before the start of the battle, Custer had ordered Reno to charge his battalion down the valley toward the Indian village about two miles ahead, explicitly promising him that his own two larger battalions of over 200 men would soon come to his assistance. As Reno and his men approached the village, they encountered an unexpectedly strong force of warriors, which succeeded in turning the battalion's flank and threatened to encircle the entire command. Reno ordered a temporary retreat to the protection of a timbered area nearby, finally making a charge to the relative safety of a bluff top about a mile away. Custer's promised support was nowhere to be seen, leaving the increasingly desperate soldiers praying for salvation by the celebrated "general" and cursing him for the unending delay.

No one suspected the real reason for his failure to appear. While Porter toiled in his field hospital and Reno's men contended with a seemingly endless hail of bullets from well-armed Indians encircling the base of their hilltop position, just four miles to the north Custer and all the men in his battalions lay dead. One warrior later remarked that it had only taken as long to kill every soldier in Custer's command as it took to enjoy a good meal—about forty-five minutes.[4]

As Porter approached the witness chair, he bore the hardened memories of soldiers who had survived under his care as well as those who had been beyond his rescue. Long-range Indian sniper bullets too often hit their marks. Thirst and dehydration took their toll too, especially among the wounded. And because medical treatment in 1876 could not yet address that most insidious of killers, infection, Porter's skillful surgeries often could not prevent wounded men from dying.

If requested by court members or lawyers, Porter was willing to dredge up the desperate circumstances within that precarious hilltop redoubt, where many of the soldiers were terrorized by the thought of being overrun by "savages" believed to torture—by scalping, cutting, and riddling with arrows—before they killed. The military witnesses who had appeared already had been careful to provide generalized responses, voicing the incontestable opinion that had Reno in fact behaved like a coward—as alleged by the prosecution—none of them would now be sitting in the courtroom. The surgeon understood that his own candid testimony, delivered under oath and likely to contain more detail, might work at odds with Reno's defense. Indeed, his statements might serve to further tarnish the reputation of the entire Seventh Cavalry. As Henry Porter took the witness chair on that frigid winter afternoon, he braced himself as he prepared to revisit the Battle of the Little Big Horn.

Part I

Engagements

1

Fateful Decisions

THE SEVENTH REGIMENT OF U.S. CAVALRY, all twelve companies together for the first time since the unit's formation after the Civil War, advanced during a march lasting from just after midnight to daylight. On June 25, 1876, daylight arrived at that eastern Montana latitude as early as 2:30 in the morning. In the initial darkness, men, horses, and pack mules filed along, guided only by the soft clanking of metallic gear ahead and behind. These accouterments did not include the cavalrymen's trademark sabers: Lieutenant Colonel Custer had ordered them left behind at the camp near the mouth of the Powder River. The famous Seventh Cavalry band also remained behind on June 22 after it played the regimental song, "Garry Owen," for the thirty-one officers, 566 enlisted men, thirty-five Indian scouts, thirteen quartermaster employees, two civilians, and 140-mule pack train, all departing under Custer's personal command. Some enlisted men and civilian admirers still referred to their commander as General Custer—he had earned the rank of major general by brevet and appointment during the Civil War. The lieutenant colonel had ordered the march in the dark, quiet early hours of June 25, moving along Davis Creek and up the hilly divide that separated his regiment from the valley of the Little Big Horn River. The plan was to summit the Wolf Mountains quickly and then rest on the other side.[1]

Stealth also guided 2nd Lieutenant Charles Varnum, Chief Scout

Charlie "Lonesome" Reynolds, and nearly a dozen Arikara or Ree Indian scouts on a separate night ride to a high spur called the Crow's Nest, a vantage point known by the Crow Indians, who conveniently hid there after they had stolen horses from their mortal enemies, the Sioux. The scouts hoped that in the clarity of the cool morning air, the view from the Crow's Nest would reveal wisps of smoke rising from the Sioux village they suspected to find in the Little Big Horn Valley. As dawn approached, every man strained to locate the anticipated village some fifteen miles away. While Lieutenant Varnum had difficulty seeing far distances in the dim early morning light, his Indian scouts were able to recognize a very large herd of ponies. Varnum's skepticism that any living thing could be detected at such a distance prompted the Rees to adjust his sights, telling him to "look for worms" in the grass instead of horses on a hillside.[2]

When Varnum's messengers found Custer shortly afterward, the regiment had halted along the trail for a four-to-five-hour rest and a soldier's breakfast of raw bacon, hardtack, and canteen water. A few fires were started for coffee. Custer himself reached the Crow's Nest at around 9:00 A.M., when the more moisture-laden midmorning air made it impossible to see the "worms" in the distant grass. Even using Lieutenant Charles DeRudio's Austrian-made field glasses, the lieutenant colonel never saw the huge pony herd that the scouts insisted was a sign of an immense enemy village. The Ree had understood the importance of the pony numbers. Bloody Knife, Custer's favorite scout, predicted that a fight with such a large number of Sioux in the valley could last three days; Charlie Reynolds warned that below them was the greatest encampment of hostiles that he had ever seen on the Upper Missouri; and Mitch Boyer, a mixed-blood Sioux, personalized the odds: "If you don't find more Indians in that valley than you ever saw together before," he declared, "you can hang me." But the genuine concern of the scouts seemed to fall on deaf ears. While Custer accepted the reports of the village location, he dismissed the warnings about its size. He even berated several scouts as cowards.[3]

The regiment continued to march up Davis Creek until just after 10:00 A.M., when Custer, Varnum, and the scouts rejoined the command. Now armed with the knowledge of the Sioux village's location, Custer considered moving his troops even closer to ready them for an attack in the early morning of June 26. This plan was still consistent with the strategy outlined several days earlier by Brigadier General Alfred Terry, commander of the expedition. He had ordered the Seventh Cavalry to ride south, scouting upriver on Rosebud Creek; traverse to the Little Big Horn River; and then move north, pushing downriver on June 25. In so doing, Custer would act as the southern pincer in coordination with the northern pincer, soldiers under Terry and Colonel John Gibbon—commanding officer of the Montana column—marching south from the Yellowstone River and advancing up the Little Big Horn. Together they would squeeze the encamped Sioux into submission and eventual relocation onto their designated reservation. But for the second time that morning, Custer received some unwelcome news: the detection of his column by roving Sioux scouts. Stripped of the element of surprise, the early morning attack planned for the next day was stillborn. Custer had to reconsider his options. Most men in the command, though still unaware of their commander's rapidly changing plans, abruptly learned that he had reached some decision. More precisely, they *heard* the decision in the form of a bugle sounding officers' call: the first bugle call since they had departed from their Yellowstone River camp three days earlier.[4]

As the sound of the bugle pierced the enforced quiet of the military camp, all officers hurried to receive orders. Among them was thirty-year-old assistant surgeon George Edwin Lord. An 1871 graduate of the Chicago Medical College, Lord was initially appointed acting assistant, or contract surgeon, by the U.S. Army in the same year. As such, he joined the group of civilian doctors hired under specific, temporary "contracts": as noncommissioned medical officers, they had no permanent military rank or authority. But Lord had ambition exceeding this status, so he took the highly rigorous Army Medical Board examination in 1875. Of the four candidates before the board's examiners, two withdrew and one failed: only George Lord passed the grueling weeklong test, for which the general failure rate was well over 50 percent. Lord was commissioned into the army in June 1875 and appointed assistant surgeon with the rank of first lieutenant. After three years of service, he would automatically be promoted to captain and thereafter achieve the rank of major if a vacancy occurred due to resignation or death. Significant pay increases and eligibility for a pension accompanied all promotions. A decidedly handsome career lay ahead of him.[5]

Lord had served as post surgeon at Fort Buford before the onset of this campaign and was detailed to the Seventh Cavalry on June 15. But on the morning of the twenty-fifth, his service was jeopardized by a physical condition not uncommon to military men serving in the field—"trail colic." The senior captain of the regiment, Frederick Benteen, took note of Lord's condition just two days earlier, when the surgeon straggled into camp very late, completely tired out from the march and refusing any food and water. The infection causing the characteristic bowel cramps and diarrhea was also known as "summer cholera," or dysentery. Most likely his condition resulted from drinking the often acrid-tasting water tainted by the runoff of salts from the soils. The purgative effect was debilitating and often excruciating. It was not uncommon for horses to refuse to drink such alkaline water, which even fouled a pot of strong coffee. Assistant Surgeon Lord would have treated himself with tincture of opium, paregoric, or the widely accepted favorite palliative of whiskey.[6]

Custer was well aware of the doctor's condition. Despite the fact that Lord held an officer's rank while the other two surgeons accompanying the regiment were noncommissioned and technically without any rank, he nevertheless suggested that Lord remain with the rear guard when the cavalry advanced into battle. Custer favored another surgeon, one he considered to be an excellent rider, as Lord's replacement in his fighting column. Acting Assistant Surgeon Henry Porter thus was summoned and presented with an unforeseen opportunity. But Lord never wavered in military discipline and commitment to his post—it was unthinkable not to ride with the famed commander of the Seventh Cavalry. Whatever physical discomfort he experienced on the morning of June 25, Lord willed it away convincingly enough, standing his ground opposite Porter, his junior in age, and, more importantly, as a contract surgeon, his lesser in status. Custer acquiesced, assigning Lord to ride with him and Porter to serve with Major Reno's battalion.[7]

At 11:45 in the morning, the entire regiment moved out, halting once more just after crossing the mountainous divide between Rosebud Creek and the Little Big Horn. It was 12:07 P.M. according to the watches set to Chicago time, the standard officers observed even in eastern Montana since regional time zones had not yet been established; the actual time of day was almost ninety minutes earlier. Custer had reached the critical decision to launch an immediate attack on the Sioux village: waiting until the next morning—a more conventional time for a surprise attack—risked finding the Indians no longer camped in that location. But this meant that his soldiers would fight without the originally planned aid of the Terry and Gibbon column pressing down from the north. Supremely confident, the lieutenant colonel ordered his regiment divided into four fighting battalions under the commands of Captain Myles Keogh, Captain George Yates, Captain Benteen, and Major Reno. Captain Thomas McDougall and Company B took charge of the 140-mule pack train. Assistant Surgeon Lord lined up with the five companies under Keogh and Yates when Custer announced that he would ride with them. Contract surgeons Porter and James DeWolf received orders to serve with Reno's battalion of three companies. Benteen's battalion, also composed of three companies, did not merit an accompanying surgeon.[8]

Custer made these fateful decisions without the benefit of sufficient military intelligence. He was not convinced of the enormous size of the village below as presaged by his scouts. Experience had shown that Indians would rather scatter and retreat prudently than fight and suffer the loss of hard-to-replace warriors. It was the prospect of Indians scattering, not fighting, that caused him anxiety. The resolve of the tribes encamped in the Little Big Horn Valley—perhaps the most important piece of intelligence—was still entirely unknown to Custer, Terry, and Gibbon alike. News that many of the warriors, Sioux and Cheyenne, had already clashed with Brigadier General George Crook's soldiers on June 17 at the Rosebud Creek had not yet reached the other two military columns. That engagement and an earlier battle on March 17 had put the tribes on notice and resulted in a powerful alliance between the Northern Cheyenne and the Sioux. The Battle of the Rosebud, which had occurred only about thirty miles southeast of Custer's present position, had at best ended in a draw. Crook insisted on calling it a victory, while more than 800 Sioux and Cheyenne warriors rode off to enjoy their own victory feast, convinced that they had outbattled an army force of 1,000 men or more. The Indians then carried their jubilation and confidence to the Little Big Horn, where that ardor fueled their fierce determination to resist all forces threatening their centuries-old way of life. Although he was about to descend upon and attack a village teeming with families, Custer could not have anticipated the unwavering ferocity of the protective warriors that his Seventh Cavalry would shortly confront.[9]

In the ninety-degree heat of that June day, the Seventh Cavalry sat momentarily poised on the divide between the Rosebud and the Little Big Horn. Nearly seventy years earlier, Lewis and Clark first named these waters, which flow from south to north and empty into the larger Yellowstone River. On this same Sunday afternoon, the U.S. Centennial Exhibition commanded the attention of large crowds in Philadelphia, celebrating the declaration of the nation's independence one hundred years earlier. This historic and joyous anniversary enamoring crowds in the East was the occasion for a historic confrontation on the western plains, where two incompatible cultures were about to collide.[10] The desire for freedom—interpreted differently by each culture and regarded by each as tantamount to its own survival—forged nearly every decision made from the moment the Seventh Cavalry left that hilly divide at 12:12 P.M. on June 25, 1876.

2

"The Starting of a Young M.D."

MORE THAN 5,000 CIVILIAN *contract* surgeons—designated as *acting* assistant surgeons—served in the U.S. Army during the Civil War, supplementing the services of the 6,000 or more *regular,* or commissioned, army surgeons. When the war ended, contract surgeons returned to their civilian practices. The postwar Congress, determined to reduce the size and cost of the peacetime army, practiced a fiscal austerity that included curtailing the practice of hiring or contracting with civilian surgeons. Consequently, contract surgeons could not rely on steady work and were obliged to apply annually for new agreements. As defined by the Association for Acting Assistant Surgeons, these men had no rank, no uniform, and no claim to a pension or final resting place in a national cemetery.[1]

None of this bothered twenty-four-year-old Henry Porter in 1872, when he graduated from the two-year program at Georgetown Medical School. He and his twenty classmates faced a shortage of opportunities to practice their art among the many already established civilian surgeons—synonymously referred to as physicians at that time since surgery as a separate medical specialty had not yet been established. Competition for patients even dissuaded Porter from trying to practice with his own physician father, Henry Norton Porter, in New York Mills, a town in central New York. Many young doctors thus looked to the West for opportunities. The increasing flow of settlers westward and the building of the railroads demanded greater protective service from the army, fracturing its forces across a geographically disparate array of posts and camps. By 1874 the army had been reduced to just over 25,000 men. Its medical department reflected equally sharp reductions. Despite the hiring limitations dictated by Congress, the army could not avoid contracting with civilian surgeons for service at its nearly two hundred military posts and with all military detachments sent out into the field. But the numbers of these hired surgeons continued to drop sharply, from 2,000 in 1865 to 262 in 1866, 187 in 1870, and finally to a quota of only 75 in 1874.[2]

Within three months of receiving his medical degree, luck favored Henry Porter, who signed his first contract with the U.S. Army on June 26, 1872, for $125 a month and including rations, transportation, and accommodations. While the *commissioned* army surgeons were often sent to relatively desirable locations for duty, noncommissioned contract surgeons more commonly were dispatched to remote areas with harsh climates. Porter headed by train across the country to the Presidio of San Francisco, headquarters of the Division of the Pacific, early in July 1872. It was his first stop en route to his ordered destination: Fort Whipple, near the town of Prescott, Arizona Territory. At every planned stopover along the way, Porter confirmed his orders in formal letters to J. K. Barnes, surgeon general, U.S. Army. He opened each letter conventionally with the phrase, "I have the honor to report . . . ," and closed each one with equal courtesy: "Very respectfully, Your Obedient servant, H. R. Porter, Acting Assistant Surgeon, U.S. Army." The young man, exuding pride in his appointment, likely anticipated little else ahead but professional opportunity and personal adventure.[3]

At Fort Whipple, Porter received specific orders to accompany a detachment of the Fifth Cavalry into the field near Camp Walapai, located forty miles northeast of Prescott. These orders came by command of Brigadier General Crook, appointed head of the Department of Arizona in 1871. Crook had devised a campaign against the

Apache Indians that drove them to higher, colder, and often snow-covered elevations under the persistent pursuit of soldiers from the Fifth Cavalry in an effort to demoralize them into accepting life on appointed reservations. Apaches traveled fast, carrying little and often wearing less, and had adapted to Arizona living. The assignment to accompany the column was well timed for Acting Assistant Surgeon Porter, who began to confess a sense of discouragement in a letter to his family: "I am heartily sick of Arizona and homesick as I have never been before. I have no chance to read or improve my medical knowledge and I wish I had never seen Arizona." In fact, he questioned the need for the very presence of the army in the territory, which he judged "as out of the way and as far from a railroad and civilization as a person can get in the United States." Nothing in the scenery—spiny cactus, thorny mesquite, or endless dust—appealed to Porter. And without a railroad, the territory was indeed isolated. Unendurable heat from a sun that, as Lieutenant John G. Bourke described it, "shone not to warm and enlighten, but to enervate and kill," drained the young doctor's enthusiasm for his army assignment. "I can't see any use in the government sending troops here to protect so miserable a country at such an enormous expense," he wrote to his parents, "better let the Indians have it."[4]

Riding along with these scouting expeditions saved Porter from the tedium of post life, where some men killed time by engineering battles between nests of red and black ants. As the soldiers moved higher in elevation and away from the searing heat of the vast Arizona desert, life again became tolerable for a short time. But a scouting expedition under Crook's command allowed few comforts. To be successful, an Indian-fighting army had to move as quickly as its foe. To that end Crook's men traveled light, forgoing such conventional equipment as tents, cots, and extra clothing. The soldiers suffered from the dramatic changes in temperature and climate as they ascended into the mountains. Porter recorded details about sleeping on the frigid, sometimes snowy, ground under a single blanket and rising at 2:00 A.M. for a 4:00 A.M. departure. As they walked their horses over rocky terrain where the animals could not be ridden, the men felt the steepness of the trails in their own muscles and in the tension of their nerves, while the loose stones underfoot tested their sore ankles and blistered feet. It was not uncommon to wear out a pair of shoes climbing the rough terrain, crisscrossed by numerous ravines and arroyos. But of all the threats posed by the environment, the army recognized thirst and dehydration as perhaps the most severe. Porter once survived a harrowing forty-eight hours in the field when his column's Walapai scouts could not locate any watering holes. Had they come upon a band of Apache warriors, the desperate men would not have felt any more endangered than they already did in that parched, godforsaken terrain. On October 7 Porter issued a bleak assessment of his station in life: "I think there is nothing in the world so difficult and so discouraging as the starting of a young M.D."[5]

Henry Porter had hoped to earn and save some money from his army contract in order to start a medical practice—anywhere, evidently, but in Arizona Territory. Finally, after fourteen months of service in Crook's relentless campaign, the surgeon applied to end his contract. He would leave with the personal satisfaction of having participated in two significant fights. The first of these occurred in late September 1872, shortly after he arrived. Porter rode with the Fifth Cavalry and witnessed its attack on Apaches in Muchos Canyon, adjacent to the Santa Maria River. The army suffered no fatal casualties, but some forty Apaches were killed, and the remaining Indians were so intimidated that, as General Crook noted, "hostilities ceased in that section of the country." In January 1873, again with companies of the Fifth Cavalry, Porter endured a night climb into the wilderness of the Superstition Mountains for the purpose of surprising a rancheria of Apaches at dawn. The warriors escaped, leaving noncombatants—an old chief, women, and children—to be taken captive by the soldiers. Crook considered it a successful engagement. "The examples of personal exertion and daring among the officers and men, if all told, would fill a volume," a proud Crook wrote in his annual report of 1872–73. As the medical officer in the field with the column, Porter could rightfully claim a share of the general's praise.[6]

At Porter's request, the army formally annulled his contract on August 25, 1873. Arizona Territory never endeared itself to the physician, but the arduous scouting expeditions and battles conditioned him to be able to "ride fifty miles or walk fifteen, over mountains and through canyons, as well as any of the old soldiers." He also earned an invaluable commendation. From Headquarters, Department of Arizona, on April 9, 1873, Crook had cited Porter in General Order No. 14: "Dr. Porter is honorably mentioned for gallantry at the engagements in the Superstition Mountains, Arizona Territory, January 16, 1873 and for conspicuous services and gallantry in the different engagements in the closing campaign against the Tonto Apaches in February and March 1873." The young surgeon had been tested by some of the harshest conditions military life and service in the field could offer, and he had displayed physical and mental stamina.[7]

Nearly twenty years later, Lieutenant Bourke, longtime aide-de-camp to the general, wrote in his memoirs about the surgeons serving in Crook's command and included Porter by name in his acknowledgment: "There was one class of officers who were entitled to all the praise they received and much more besides, and that class was the surgeons, who never flagged in their attentions to sick and wounded, whether soldier or officer, American, Mexican or apache captive, by night or by day." True to his physician's oath, Porter tended to turn a blind eye to distinctions among men—being all of flesh and blood, they equally deserved a doctor's care. This scientific outlook on Porter's part was again evident when he sent his father a scalp—most likely acquired from a Walapai or Apache scout rehabilitated and now working for the army—which the elder man had expressed an interest in seeing. The two physicians, father and son, saw nothing gruesome or prize worthy in this battlefield souvenir: it was a piece of the human anatomy, of scientific interest and, it seems, nothing more.[8]

Acting Assistant Surgeon Porter left Arizona and returned to Washington, D.C., in August 1873. No doubt life in the nation's capital provided a level of comfort and social distraction absent from the life he had known the previous fourteen months. And yet on October 2, Porter wrote Surgeon General Barnes to apply for a second contract with the army. The reply reached his sister's residence at 1613 19th Street NW, where he was staying, just four days later: "No additional acting assistant surgeons are at present required."[9] But Porter's application was placed on file for future consideration. His application included a copy of the commendation in General Order No. 14 from General Crook, a reference of critical importance, he believed, for any future contracts. Porter's degree from Georgetown Medical School; his service in the remote, demanding conditions of Arizona; the written commendation from the highly respected Crook, who was notoriously austere with his praise; and even Porter's good character and health contributed to his file being classified as a "Good Record." The payoff for this status came quickly, on October 16, in the form of the offer of a second contract at $100 a month. This time the army stationed Porter in a climate more to his liking, ordering him to proceed to Saint Paul, Minnesota, and report to the Medical Director's Office at Headquarters, Department of Dakota, for assignment to duty.

For Porter, life with the army was enterprising and seemingly advantageous to his career in medicine. He had secured not one but two contracts in the face of congressional limitations placed on the army's medical service; his tenure in the demanding Arizona Territory procured a rare commendation from a most respected general; and he was headed west once again not only to practice his art but also to satisfy an ardent sense of adventure. The army obliged him in October 1873 with the assignment of post surgeon at Camp Hancock, Dakota Territory, to minister to the medical needs of the soldiers garrisoning this important quartermaster depot at the Northern Pacific Railroad terminus at Bismarck.

His duties, concerned mostly with camp hygiene, often proved tedious, but the location of the camp, in a part of newly founded Bismarck and across the Missouri River from Fort Abraham Lincoln, was promising for other opportunities. By December 1874 Porter requested a release from his army contract as his ambitions broadened and his attention turned to establishing "Nicholson & Porter, Druggists and Stationers" in town. Bismarck could boast of a Northern Pacific Railroad depot, a telegraph office just across the tracks, and much activity at its wharves edging the Missouri River, where steamboats landed and launched with cargo and passengers. Bismarck, at least in its fair-weather months, was hardly isolated. The Northern Pacific, in 1872, had laid out the original city grid on the hills overlooking the river. Within a year, 147 buildings, most wooden and many with false fronts, hugged the often muddy dirt streets.[10] Settlers from Norway, Sweden, and Germany—frequently moving south from the British Possessions (modern Canada)—came mostly for the farming opportunities that the flat, open land provided. The railroad would help move their crops of wheat to market.

Economically, Bismarck was thriving as it housed the crews building the railroad. In response to the company's promotional campaign and its widely disseminated message—"Men are needed in Dakota"—native-born Americans and immigrants newly arrived from Northern and Central Europe gravitated to the area. They were "unskilled, unlettered, but willing" to work a ten-hour day and sleep in tents, dugouts, or crudely constructed boarding houses.[11] These men were a rugged lot, but their valuable labor warranted the protection of the U.S. Army, and Bismarck welcomed the presence of the Seventh Cavalry to its growing clientele.

Porter's business venture proved to be short lived. Either due to a downturn in business or a personal desire to rejoin army life, the young surgeon applied for a contract in June and then again in August 1875, this time addressing his letter to Major William J. Sloan, medical director, Department of Dakota. Porter pulled out all the stops: his experience in Arizona with hard service in the field; his record on file in the Surgeon General's Office in Washington, D.C.; and—perhaps the clincher—his *permanent* residency in Bismarck. The physician had cut his teeth in the arid western landscape of Arizona Territory, and now he was coming of age in the vast plains and jutting buttes of Dakota Territory. In late September Sloan offered Porter his third contract: to "give necessary medical attendance to the troops at Camp Hancock, [applying] to the Post surgeon at Fort A. Lincoln for medical supplies." Porter responded immediately, saying, "[Sloan's] request will be most cheerfully complied with."[12] Even the compensation of sixty dollars a month was satisfactory to Porter, who quite possibly set his sights squarely on a prize that far exceeded the meager salary: proximity to and association with the Seventh Cavalry and George Armstrong Custer, the army's premier Indian fighter, who had commanded his regiment in the Washita Campaign (1868–69), the Yellowstone Expedition (1873), and the Black Hills Expedition (1874). By 1876 Custer's name had become synonymous with derring-do and adventure.

3

"Hostiles"

ONE YEAR AFTER THE UNION PACIFIC and Central Pacific Railways joined on May 10, 1869, to the sound of a celebrated golden spike being driven into a celebrated rail tie at Promontory Summit, Utah, groundbreaking for the Northern Pacific Railroad took place just west of Duluth, Minnesota. The long-held dream to unite Lake Superior with Puget Sound and the Pacific Ocean and create a railroad corridor for the transportation of goods between the East and the West had gained purchase. Three survey crews for the railroad set out in 1871, 1872, and1873. Each required a military escort as it explored routes across western Dakota and Montana Territories, trekking onto Sioux lands while measuring and mapping the territory along the Yellowstone River. By the Sioux account, areas south of the Yellowstone constituted the northern limit of the unceded land granted to them for hunting under the Fort Laramie Treaty of 1868. They thus considered the surveyors' activities a violation of the agreement. Whites saw it a different way. Genuine concerns for the safety of the men in this building project of great national importance reached the War Department in Washington. The secretary of war, General William W. Belknap, responded decisively to these fears about Indian "depredations" by deploying troops, including the Seventh Cavalry.[1]

In 1866 President Andrew Johnson and Congress had authorized the army to establish four additional regiments of cavalry—the

Seventh through the Tenth—to support two critical national policies: the Reconstruction effort in the South and the expansionist movement in the West. The president envisioned the cavalry "as a weapon against the plains Indians." To police the western territories, the Seventh was divided and stationed at seven forts throughout Kansas and Colorado. The various companies often protected crews of men building the Eastern Division of the Union Pacific Railroad, its steady westward movement a continual instigator of Kiowa, Comanche, and Southern Cheyenne resistance. The Seventh Cavalry then redeployed to the South in 1871. Again its twelve companies were scattered throughout many southern states, serving as "mounted police" primarily against the postwar activities of the Ku Klux Klan.[2]

As part of the effort to protect Northern Pacific surveyors, the Seventh Cavalry was reassigned in 1873 from the Department of the South to the Department of Dakota. The thousand-mile transfer that spring was a complex operation, requiring four separate trains to travel the distance from Cairo, Illinois, to a railroad terminus in Yankton, Dakota Territory, to transport "over 800 men and horses, hogs, and mules," plus tons of garrison and camp equipage. It was a timely move for the army, since the rails of the Northern Pacific reached the Missouri River and the city of Bismarck soon afterward in July, and the critical third survey expedition was about to explore the disputed routes across Montana Territory.[3]

Custer, again in command of the Seventh Cavalry due to the long-term absence of its colonel, Samuel D. Sturgis, relocated with his men to Yankton, then moved on to Fort Rice, Dakota Territory, to prepare for the summer-long escort of the surveyors. Only at the completion of this "Yellowstone Expedition" did the regiment return to Dakota Territory and occupy the newly rebuilt Fort Abraham Lincoln.

Fort Lincoln was unique, housing both infantry and cavalry on a large expanse of land running nearly a mile from north to south on the west bank of the Missouri River. While the infantry occupied a post built on an overlooking bluff, the cavalry buildings were situated closer to the river, making it easier to water the more than 600 horses stabled there. The cavalry officers' quarters, barracks, hospital, stables, and laundry, along with other smaller buildings, were situated around a military parade ground. The fort opened west upon the barren landscape of the Dakota prairie and east across the broad Missouri River and the city of Bismarck just upstream.[4]

Custer and the Seventh Cavalry served in a military hierarchy directly commanded by Brigadier General Alfred H. Terry, in charge of the Department of Dakota, headquartered in Saint Paul, Minnesota. From there the chain of command rose to Lieutenant General Philip H. Sheridan, commanding the Division of the Missouri, headquartered in Chicago. General William Tecumseh Sherman, commander of the army, Secretary of War William Belknap, and President Ulysses S. Grant were all based in Washington, D.C. Each had served with distinction in the Civil War.

As Custer and the Seventh Cavalry were transitioning to Dakota, issues with westward expansion were testing President Grant and his administration. Progress of the Northern Pacific Railroad was but one issue. In fact, construction of the railroad came to an abrupt halt in September 1873. Unable to sell off construction bonds and with cash reserves nearly exhausted, the company's private financier—Jay Cooke & Company—collapsed, closed the doors of its bank and branches, and brought the building of the railway to a stop. Construction would not resume for a decade. The simultaneous nationwide financial crisis—the Panic of 1873—brought the nation to an economic standstill.[5]

Meanwhile, the prospect of gold in the Black Hills of Dakota continued to loom brightly, and territorial boosters doggedly advocated for a survey to determine its potential. Disregarding the fact that the Black Hills lay amid the Great Sioux Reservation, Grant acquiesced to a survey. Custer was charged with protecting it.

By the eve of the so-called Black Hills Expedition of 1874, Grant had strayed from his long-advocated goodwill policy toward the American Indians, yielding to the priorities of western exploration and expansion in the service of the nation's economic recovery. The president consoled himself with the thought that if the government could relocate Indians from their ancestral lands onto reservations "for their own good," then western expansion would also serve as a civilizing force for these native people.[6]

Gold in the Black Hills posed a special problem for President Grant because the Fort Laramie Treaty of 1868 guaranteed to the Sioux their reservation, including the Black Hills, as an inviolable territory. Moreover, the country between the North Platte and Yellowstone Rivers and from the Big Horn Mountains east to the Dakota line was set aside as a perpetual hunting ground. The agreement also stipulated that white men could not legally trespass on these designated territories. In September 1875 the U.S. government attempted to purchase the Black Hills from the Indians, but no amount of money could match the sense of sacredness the Sioux felt for this land.[7]

For a while, Grant stood at an impasse. He could uphold the legality of the Fort Laramie Treaty and safeguard the territory from illegal miners and other trespassers, or he could bend to the compelling demands of a depressed economy and opt for much-needed gold. Ever the nationalist, the president finally endorsed a military solution of several phases. He deliberately turned a blind eye to whites trespassing onto Indian land. He also directed those Indians hunting buffalo off the formal reservation to return. If such "winter roamers," as they were called, refused to return to the reservation, they would be deemed "hostiles" and force would be brought against them. Once the Indians were identified as "hostile," responsibility for them shifted from the Interior Department to the War Department. Grant assured himself that what he was doing was for the ultimate good of the Sioux, converting them into civilized farmers safely ensconced on government reservations. He assumed the public would support this ostensible altruism.[8]

But the real key to this vision lay in the term "hostile." In truth, Indian depredations across Sioux country were at a low in 1875, and the "winter roamers," under Hunkpapa and Oglala Sioux leaders like Sitting Bull and Crazy Horse, were rightfully hunting on land accorded them in the Fort Laramie Treaty. Moreover, they hunted out of necessity since the government-promised food rations often were sporadic at best and criminally meager at worst. In what way was this behavior "hostile"? The military mindset of President Grant, Secretary of Interior Zachariah Chandler, and Secretary of War Belknap simply reformulated the question: How can we construe this roaming and hunting as "hostile" and, consequently, premise an Indian war?

With an eerie timeliness, Indian Inspector Erwin Curtis Watkins, one of only three government inspectors, had recently returned to Washington from an annual tour of the Dakota and Montana Indian agencies. He composed a report in November 1875 that condemned the activities of "certain wild and hostile bands" roaming in the unceded lands and threatening both settlers and other tribes. His conclusion prescribed "[sending] troops against them in the winter, the sooner the better, and *whip* them into subjection."[9] It is not known whether Watkins actually wrote his report or simply signed one already prepared for him. Nevertheless, his name remains synonymous with the resolution of Grant's dilemma, and the "Watkins Report" quickly led to an order from Secretary Chandler to all Sioux agents on December 6: Locate all the winter roamers in unceded territories and require them to return to a reservation by January 31, 1876. Those who did not comply with the mandate would be labeled "hostiles" and become subject to military pursuit.

On the basis of a single official document of dubious reasoning and veracity, Grant, Chandler, Belknap, and Generals Sheridan and Crook had arrived at a rationale for ending the "Indian problem" through military means. The ultimatum reached the agencies at Red Cloud and Spotted Tail in Nebraska; Standing Rock, Cheyenne River, Lower Brule, Crow Creek, and Devil's Lake in Dakota Territory; and Fort Peck in Montana Territory. Although agents could not reconcile their personal knowledge of the currently peaceful Indian behavior with the notion of a strong military threat implied in the mandate, they nevertheless sent runners out to find the winter camps along the Yellowstone River and the tributaries snaking from it. The messengers did not reach some of the remote camps until as late as January 21, ten days before the deadline. In any case, it was not at all surprising that the order failed to bring any Indians back to the reservation. The government had contrived an impossible deadline, and even if any roamers were so inclined to return, heavy snows impeded virtually all travel.

By January 1876 the Indians in the winter bands largely understood three things: They could not realistically comply with the mandate and reach the agencies by the set date. Moreover, most would not consider obeying the demand, knowing that they were rightfully hunting on unceded lands. But most important, the demeanor of the government had changed sharply. A perfect storm of colliding interests was gathering on the northern plains.

General Sherman and his protégé in the West, Phil Sheridan, envisioned an approach against the "hostile" Indians resembling the recently successful campaign used in the Red River War in Texas and Oklahoma Territory in 1874–75. Army columns would relentlessly pursue and continually uproot the bands of nonreservation Indians, depriving them of the opportunity to hunt and replenish food supplies, ultimately starving them onto the reservation or even into the afterlife. General Sheridan's maxim—"protection for the good, punishment for the bad"—now had a government sanction and military force behind it.[10]

4

The Dakota Column

ACTING ASSISTANT SURGEON HENRY PORTER had fulfilled his third contract with the army, serving as post surgeon at Camp Hancock during the late fall and winter of 1875 and into the spring of 1876. Since 1872 the camp had housed infantrymen variously protecting supplies and workers assigned to the construction of the Northern Pacific Railroad as well as quartermaster supplies destined for posts throughout the upper Missouri region. Porter had eagerly assumed the medical care of the Seventeenth Infantry company in his charge. By 1874, the population of nearby Bismarck was estimated at about 1,200 people, and the city advertised its critical location both as the temporary endpoint of the Northern Pacific and as a major port for all the steamboat traffic navigating the Missouri River. To Porter, Camp Hancock, Fort Abraham Lincoln, and Bismarck represented an exciting opportunity, however rough and tumble these places may have been. His future colleague on the Little Big Horn Campaign, James DeWolf, lately of Fort Totten, Dakota Territory, took a less rosy view of the city, writing to his wife on April 16, 1876, shortly after he arrived: "Bismarck is a squalid dunghill sort of place. All wooden buildings."[1]

When the construction of the Northern Pacific was suspended indefinitely in 1873 for lack of funding, the mission of the troops stationed in the region shifted in accordance with the government's plan for dealing with the newly deemed "hostile" Indians.

Throughout the late winter and spring of 1876, Porter witnessed the campaign preparations—ever increasing numbers of cavalry, infantry, and horses, and the amassing of supplies—until the shift to an offensive posture became apparent and then public. The full deployment was ultimately revealed in the heading of Porter's fourth contract with the army on May 15, 1876: "In compliance with General Field Orders No. 5 . . . I have this day been assigned to duty with the *Expedition against hostile Sioux.*"[2] The signatures of approval on the contract—Brigadier General Terry, Surgeon General Barnes, and Surgeon William J. Sloan, medical director of the Department of Dakota—indicated the significance of the expedition.

Army command envisioned a three-column convergence against the targeted Indians: a column from Wyoming under Brigadier General Crook, then commanding the Department of the Platte, departed Fort Fetterman on the North Platte River on March 1; a column from Montana under John Gibbon, colonel of the Seventh Infantry, set forth from Fort Ellis, three miles from Bozeman, on March 30; and a column under Terry, commander of the Department of Dakota, marched from Fort Abraham Lincoln on May 17. General Sheridan had initially planned a winter campaign against the Sioux that capitalized on three conditions: the element of surprise, heavy winter snows to impede any Indian flight, and the weak winter condition of Indian ponies, whose supply of prairie grasses was at best sparse or completely buried beneath the snow. Unexpectedly, the weather worked in the Indians' favor, when blizzards in Dakota delayed the delivery of supplies for Terry's expedition and prevented his column from departing until mid-May.

Sheridan outlined the tasks of the three military columns in a letter to Sherman. Terry would drive the Indians west toward the Big Horn River, Crook would prevent them from heading south, and Gibbon would impede any flight across the Yellowstone River heading north. If all went according to this loosely imagined plan, the three forces would "whip [the hostiles] into subjection," sending them back to the agencies and out of the way of prospectors in the Black Hills and surveyors and workers for the railroad.[3]

The numbers in each column were considerable. Colonel Gibbon left Fort Ellis with twenty-seven officers, 409 enlisted men, twenty-five Crow scouts, four quartermaster scouts, ten teamsters and two packers. The Wyoming column under Crook initially consisted of thirty-two officers, 662 enlisted men, 80 supply wagons with eighty-four civilian teamsters, five horse-drawn ambulances with a driver each, a pack train of 50 mules with 62 civilian packers, and a herd of 45 cattle. After a battle on March 17 on the Powder River, mostly with Northern Cheyenne Indians, Crook's troops returned to Fort Fetterman out of concern for the wounded and in need of supplies. When he set out again on May 29, Crook commanded fifty-one officers, 1,000 enlisted men, a pack train of 81 men and 250 mules, and a wagon train of 106 wagons and 116 men. Meanwhile, General Terry assembled in his Dakota column all twelve companies of the Seventh Cavalry—about 700 men—three infantry companies of about 140 men, three Gatling guns serviced by 32 men, 166 wagons, 45 pack mules, and a herd of 110 Texas cattle. Together the three commanders—Terry, Crook, and Gibbon—coordinated an operation of some 3,500 soldiers, which represented nearly 13 percent of the army's total strength.[4]

All of Fort Lincoln assembled to watch the departure of Terry's column on May 17 and enjoy the regimental band playing the lively "Garry Owen," the title of an Irish drinking song so loved by Custer. Small children imitated the passing soldiers, beating on tin pans and waving handkerchiefs like flags. The antics helped their mothers—wives of the departing men—maintain their composure. But soon the band struck up "The Girl I Left Behind," with the lyric, "If ever I get off the trail and Indians don't find me, I'll make my way straight back to the gal I left behind me." At the sound of those words, the women shed tears, a clear sign of their apprehension about the safety of their men. Among those departing was Acting Assistant Surgeon

Porter, who together with Acting Assistant Surgeons DeWolf, Elbert J. Clark, and Isaiah H. Ashton made up the column's medical service under the command of Assistant Surgeon John W. Williams, chief medical officer on the expedition. The assignments of the contract surgeons divided between the cavalry and the infantry. DeWolf administered to the Seventh Cavalry's right wing, Clark to the left wing. Ashton was assigned to the infantry battalion, while Porter served the headquarters and the Gatling battery.[5]

Odometers attached to the wheels of the four-mule wagon carrying the chief engineer, 1st Lieutenant Edward Maguire, recorded the distance covered by the Dakota column between May 17 and June 11: more than 320 miles from Fort Lincoln to the point at which the Powder River enters the Yellowstone. Soldiers rose for reveille around 4:00 A.M. and covered from 10 to 40 miles in a day. The weather was seasonally unpredictable, with days full of the sweet smell of prairie grass and the singing of meadowlarks alternating with sudden storms. Hail the size of hickory nuts tore holes in the canvas of the covered wagons, raised welts on the skin of the men, and terrified all the animals. On June 1 a snowstorm forced the column to remain in camp for two days. When the journey continued, the spatial monotony was broken only by the many buttes pushing skyward. Two in particular—the Sentinel Buttes—heralded the beginning of the Little Missouri Badlands that border both sides of the broad, broken valley cut into the prairie plateau by the Little Missouri River. Lieutenant Maguire likened the fiery red clay of the torturous ravines and perpendicular bluffs to the "ruins of some great city destroyed by fire." Undistracted by this foreign landscape, General Terry zigzagged his column forward. Cottonwoods brought welcome shade as the men approached the Little Missouri, but the men and the animals were punished by the grueling climb of many miles through the scoured terrain west of the river. Afterward the country opened again, allowing easier passage as the column coursed west over alternating plateaus and broad valleys toward the Powder River, the first of the major tributaries of the Yellowstone.[6]

Thus far, demands on the medical staff were light. The surgeons attended to cases of a dislocated hand, a hand abscess, an accidental self-inflicted gunshot wound to the foot, constipation, and consumption. Poisonous snakebites, although an infrequent occurrence, were a constant threat as rattlesnakes abounded in the prairie grasses. At each selected campsite, soldiers formed a skirmish line the width of a designated area, marching forward in line—slow and steady—slashing at the grass with sticks and cavalry sabers or shooting with revolvers to clear the area of unwelcome reptiles. The sweep, nearly always thorough and successful, did on one occasion result in a nasty bite. Doctors Williams and Porter responded to the unlucky victim and employed whiskey to counter the effects of the poison, a balm administered not topically on the puncture site but rather by plying the patient with twenty-six ounces.[7] After two hours of drunken stupor, the man revived with no evident ill effects from the venom. Soldiers who witnessed the cure might almost wish to suffer snakebite themselves. Between these calls to duty, the surgeons enjoyed the long marches, good suppers, and musical performances of the band every evening: almost a holiday atmosphere.

For Porter, who could still easily conjure up the memories of discomfort and hardship during the campaigns under General Crook in Arizona, life as a contract surgeon with the "Expedition against hostile Sioux" must have been satisfying. In camp he spent time with fellow surgeon James DeWolf. Both young men, aged twenty-eight and thirty-three respectively, sought service in the military as a way to practice their medical art and simply to earn a living. DeWolf had gone one step further than Porter, though. After graduating from Harvard Medical School on June 25, 1875, he immediately applied to take the exam of the Army Medical Board. At thirty-two DeWolf was technically overage for the exam, which required that candidates be between twenty-one and twenty-eight years of age. Making an exception, in August the board "invited him to appear for the examination."[8] As it happened, he failed the test. In a clever counter, however, DeWolf immediately requested that the army hire him as a contract surgeon. In less than a month, he began his one-year contract at Fort Totten, near Devil's Lake northeast of Bismarck, Department of Dakota, for $100 a month, to be increased by $25 a month when he was on the march and in the field. Like Porter, DeWolf could serve only on a temporary basis, vulnerable to discharge at the army's discretion. But with life as agreeable as it was so far on this expedition, the two young doctors could find no grounds for complaint.

Waiting at Fort Totten, Fanny Downing DeWolf received thirty-two letters from her husband during the march of the Dakota column toward the Yellowstone. The surgeon regaled his wife with tales of the pleasantries of military life, punctuated by reassurances about his safety: "I am now somewhat inclined to think our stay up here will be short. We have not seen an Indian yet nor much signs and everyone of the Command except a few think we will not find them on fighting terms." DeWolf was parroting to his wife what he had heard in camp. By June 21, when Terry's column had reached the river and the mouth of Rosebud Creek, the prevailing opinion, DeWolf wrote, was that "the Indians have scattered and gone back to their reservations." His last letter, written before marching off with the Seventh Cavalry and Custer, ended with a confident prediction: "I think it is very clear that we shall not see an Indian this summer." James DeWolf might have been a fine surgeon, but he proved to be a very poor judge of changing winds.[9]

Part II

Trials

5

"A Battle in Three Fights"

SOLDIERS AND HORSES, tired from long days of travel and a recent night march, moved down the western slope of the hilly divide between Rosebud Creek and the Little Big Horn River, picking their way across the steep, broken ground. It was shortly after noon on June 25, and the sun blazed fiercely. Custer halted his command as soon as it reached the level ground of the valley. Scouts Mitch Boyer and Charlie Reynolds had just returned from a reconnaissance ride ahead of the main column. Custer summoned them for a brief parley, then tore a piece of paper from 1st Lieutenant William W. Cooke's pocket notebook and began sketching his plan of attack on the Indian village. Most importantly, he wanted to catch the Indians unprepared to fight. Anticipating that the surprised inhabitants would immediately scatter in various directions, Custer divided his regiment by battalion: each would approach the village from different directions. If his men could ride down the fleeing noncombatants—wives, children, and elders—and gather them under the army's control, the warriors, he felt sure, would relinquish the fight.[1]

Custer organized his regiment in trident form while still twelve miles away from the village. The left prong consisted of Captain Benteen, five officers, and 110 men of Companies D, H, and K. Major Reno's battalion represented the center prong, made up of Companies A, G, and M: eleven officers, 129 men, and thirty-five others, including most of the scouts and the two contract surgeons,

DeWolf and Porter. Combining the last two battalions under the respective commands of Captains Keogh and Yates, Custer assigned to them Companies C, E, F, I, and L, totaling thirteen officers, 200 men, and eight others, including Assistant Surgeon George Lord. Custer rode at the head of this last prong. Bringing up the rear was 1st Lieutenant Edward Mathey, in charge of the 140-mule pack train, escorted by Captain Thomas McDougall and Company B. The train was hardly an afterthought, for all officers knew that the success of the imminent attack might depend in large degree on its rapid and steady progress, especially of those mules carrying the reserve ammunition.[2]

The flags of the Seventh Cavalry, guidons of stars and stripes for each of the twelve companies, stood out against the clear, midday Montana sky. Custer's personal flag was swallowtail in shape and ornamented with two crossed white sabers set against a background of horizontal red and blue stripes, fashioned of silk by Custer's wife, Libbie.[3] The lieutenant colonel knew he defied convention by attacking in the middle of the day, his preparations and tactics unaided by the cover of darkness. But his basic plan was still in concert with General Terry's design. The Seventh Cavalry would serve as the "hammer" forcing the Indians down the Little Big Horn River in a northerly direction toward the Big Horn River and the "anvil" of forces commanded by Terry and Colonel Gibbon. Custer had to make certain that no Indians escaped to the south or west. Captain Benteen's battalion—the left prong of the deployment—would serve to prevent this possibility.

At 12:12 P.M., on Sunday, June 25, Custer sent Benteen and his battalion by the left oblique to the southwest, determined not to overlook the possibility of being surprised by even more Indians encamped to the south. Benteen's orders were to ride to and beyond a line of bluffs, pitching into any hostile force he came onto, and report back by messenger. Privately, the captain considered this a senseless order, pitching in and reporting—or as he thought of it, "valley hunting ad infinitum."[4] Under such orders, Benteen and his men could travel five miles out, far enough away from the remainder of the regiment to be of no help and possibly to become isolated and imperiled. The smaller size of his battalion and the lack of an assigned surgeon insinuated to the forty-two-year-old Civil War veteran that he was being sidelined. Being a good officer, however, he followed orders, and set out valley hunting.

Also at 12:12 P.M., Major Reno and Custer led their battalions in parallel along opposite banks of a creek some ten to fifteen yards wide. Like Benteen, Reno knew no details of the battle plan. The major headed his battalion, Henry Porter riding to his left and battalion adjutant Benjamin Hodgson to his right. During the approach to the village, Reno asked Porter if he was armed. The surgeon's negative reply prompted Reno to offer him the carbine he was carrying across the pommel of his saddle.[5] He respectfully declined but may also have sensed the point of the offer: Reno needed armed combatants. The fact that Porter headed into battle unarmed suggests one more instance of misjudgment about the situation ahead. Most likely, the young surgeon expected to be a complete noncombatant in any fighting, his attention focused instead on the care of the wounded. Moreover, under the mantle of the Seventh Cavalry, the risk of personal danger seemed slight. Confidence in Custer's ability and the army's conviction that the Indians would shrink from any fight only compounded this illusion of security.

No matter how many Indians he anticipated in the valley ahead, Custer continually worried that they would get away. When the Indian trail the cavalry followed gradually widened, he suspected that the Indians were parting, with various bands dragging their lodge poles in divergent directions. But for a second time that day, Custer's scouts divined otherwise: the truth was that the trail had grown wider because, very recently, ever more Indians had reached the already expansive encampment along the Little Big Horn. People from the Great Sioux Reservation—the "summer roamers"—were arriving in numbers to join the "winter roamers," and the village had grown beyond anyone's realistic expectation or imagination.

Again Custer dismissed the scouts' interpretation of the trail and their warning of what was ahead. He so feared Indian dispersion and loss of a battle opportunity that when the Crow scout White-Man-Runs-Him observed a large dust cloud ahead, the immediate conclusion was that the Sioux were running away. Scout and interpreter Frederick Gerard shouted, "Here are your Indians, running like devils!"[6] Custer, believing that his anxiety about scattering had been confirmed, quickly abandoned any plans of waiting for Benteen's battalion and the pack train, still many miles to the rear. Immediately he sent regimental adjutant William Cooke to Reno with orders to move at a rapid gait and charge the Indians ahead. Riding alongside the major, Porter observed the exchange and watched as Reno turned carefully to ask Lieutenant Cooke if Custer was going to support him. The adjutant responded affirmatively that the lieutenant colonel would indeed support him, and then rode back to Custer's column.

At a trot Porter continued to ride to the left of Reno for over a mile until they reached the Little Big Horn and crossed over to the other side. The day being very hot, they took time to water their horses. About ten minutes later, Reno formed the command into a line, and Porter heard him give the order, "Forward!" The battalion advanced with increasing speed for about two miles down the valley toward the Indian village.

It came into view slowly, appearing in glimpses between the cottonwoods lining the river. But for every glimpse of what seemed to be an endless expanse of lodges—some 1,000 by Porter's estimate—an enormous dust cloud served to obscure the village. The immense herd of ponies—those "worms in the grass" espied much earlier in the day from the Crow's Nest—had grazed so well in the valley in previous days that the grass-stripped ground now threw up a cover of dust that enabled the Indians to hide their defensive movements.

As warriors ran ponies back and forth continuously, others directed women, children, and elders to flee from the approaching soldiers. These noncombatants abandoned the southern-most end of the village and moved northerly through the order of the encamped tribes: Hunkpapa, Oglala, Minniconjou, Brule, Sans Arc, and finally Northern Cheyenne.[7] It was a gathering of well over 7,000 people, most members of the Teton Sioux tribes but also including some Northern Cheyenne and Santee Sioux. The Cheyenne had fought against Crook earlier in the year, on March 17, compelling the general's initial Wyoming column to return to Fort Fetterman to reorganize. When Crook set out again he fought the Sioux to a draw at Rosebud Creek on June 17, an audacious showing of offensive resolve by the Indians. Absolutely nothing of this last battle was known to General Terry, Colonel Gibbon, or Lieutenant Colonel Custer on June 25.[8]

Into late-June the Sioux encampment along the Greasy Grass swelled with the arrival of "summer roamers" who had left the agencies throughout the spring. Well aware of the government's campaign against "hostiles," Sioux and Cheyenne in unprecedented numbers gravitated to the general summer gathering, not only to hunt buffalo all the while but also now to address the imminent crisis of their very survival. Large herds of buffalo and antelope were enough to sustain this large population. The abundant valley grasses also fed more than 10,000 Indian ponies. In the course of this time together, talk of survival hardened their resolve. Although the Indians had not expected a cavalry attack in the middle of an otherwise peaceful day, the nearly 2,000 warriors realized that their lives depended on an immediate and ferocious defense. The pony-generated dust cloud was merely the beginning of their resistence.[9]

Major Reno approached a band of timber near the southern end of the site and began to register the size of the village and the increasing number of Indians appearing on horseback. What he saw was alarming but told only half of the story: he and every other member of the Seventh Cavalry had no idea of the determination of these Sioux and Cheyenne. Conventional army assumptions about Indian warfare—the anticipated scattering and retreating—were about to be harshly overturned. Reno assessed the situation, ordered a halt, and employed his troopers in a skirmish line about 500 hundred yards from the village. His men shot more accurately when dismounted and not negotiating with excited horses. Every fourth man became a horse holder, securing the reins of three horses along with those of his own in the relative safety of the heavy timber close by. Thus the original 129 soldiers in Reno's battalion were reduced to a mere 95 participants on the skirmish line. At 3:10 P.M. the first carbine shots of the Battle of the Little Big Horn cracked through the dust-filled air.

About fifty yards away and alongside scouts Charlie Reynolds and Bloody Knife and interpreter George Herendeen, Henry Porter studied the action on the skirmish line. Ever more Indian warriors appeared as the soldiers fired and reloaded their single-shot breech-loading Springfield carbines as fast as possible. As the fighting intensified, Porter sobered to his professional responsibilities and went in search of Private William Robinson of Company M, who carried the bandages and medicines. Locating a single man proved tricky among the many horses, horse holders, and maneuvering soldiers. Assigned as the surgeon's orderly, or hospital attendant, Robinson carried a hospital knapsack of four compartments that housed instruments, dressings, and medicines. This knapsack was critical to the welfare of Reno's battalion because, at the time of this first fight, the bulk of the medical supplies for the entire regiment was still rocking side to side inside U.S. Army field surgical chests strapped onto mules in the pack train, stubbornly moving down the trail and still over an hour to the rear.[10]

Anxious as he was to find Robinson, Porter knew he could resort to his personal surgical pocket case as needed. The red-lined leather case contained the smaller tools of his trade: scalpel, straight and curved bistouries, gum lancet, tenaculum, catheter, silver-plated probe, angular scissors, forceps, and a surgeon's needle. With these instruments, some bandage material, and a vial of laudanum—opium in an alcoholic solvent—conveniently stored with the case, Porter could treat most smaller wounds and some degree of accompanying pain: nothing he had not already practiced on wounded soldiers, especially those in the fighting at Muchos Canyon in Arizona Territory. Stop the bleeding, ease the pain—the surgeon's cardinal rules.[11]

Suddenly Porter became aware of a large influx of soldiers around him. The Indians had turned the left flank of the skirmish line and threatened to encircle it, compelling Major Reno to order his men to fall back into the timber at a bend in the river to protect the battalion's rear. Large cottonwoods, interspersed with dense underbrush riddled with the paths of small animals, offered some protective cover. Reno then established a second line, still hoping to hold a defensive position until Custer arrived with the promised support. Not only were his men mightily outmanned, but the major was also well aware that the rapidly increasing number of warriors could ride and shoot accurately at the same time, something most of his troopers had not had enough practice to master and for which they were not trained. They were nearly surrounded by Indians who had made it their life's work to ride and shoot expertly: they were hunters.[12]

Porter's search for his orderly was made more difficult by the dense dust stirred up by the agitated horses and smoke from fires set by warriors intent on driving the cavalry out of their marginal cover. He overheard shouts about a wounded soldier nearby and found Private Henry Klotzbucher of Company M near the edge of the woods and tucked into some underbrush, still able to talk though in much pain. His red-stained blouse opened to reveal a mortal stomach wound. Porter knew that applying a dressing to stop the bleeding was futile, but he also realized that a dose of laudanum would ease the soldier's pain and maybe relieve his terror. While administering the opiate, he was keenly aware of Major Reno's voice shouting nearby: "We have got to get out of here, we have got to charge them!" It took an instant for Porter to register how men all around him were scrambling to find and mount their horses. There was no general bugle call, no coordinating signal to organize the charge, only what he saw as a "good deal of dust, hallooing and confusion." Within a few minutes the surgeon was left nearly alone, tending a frightened and dying man.[13]

Major Reno had tallied in his head all the factors contributing to the imminent disaster he faced. Many hundreds of warriors were gradually encircling his battalion. He had not yet received the promised support from Custer and had no idea about his commander's larger battle plan. Although aware that Captain Benteen had been ordered to pursue an oblique direction, Reno regretted not knowing more about Benteen's extended orders. The Seventh Cavalry was now divided into three fighting battalions, each seemingly cut off from effective communication with the others. Judging from the swarm of warriors, the village likely approximated the enormous size anticipated by the worried scouts. Reno knew that this was not the first time that Custer had divided his regiment and headed into battle with inadequate knowledge of the size of the targeted Indian village. He had not been at the Battle of Washita in 1868, when Custer and the Seventh Cavalry attacked a sleeping Cheyenne encampment along the Washita River in Oklahoma Territory. But thanks to persistent rumor, kept alive by one of the lieutenant colonel's harshest critics, Captain Benteen, Reno was all too aware of the fate of Major Joel Elliott and his seventeen-man detachment.[14]

Elliott and his men independently pursued a group of fleeing Indians far enough away from the main command to become isolated. The mysterious disappearance of these eighteen soldiers went unaddressed until later in the afternoon, when Custer ordered a search for them. In the growing dusk of the winter day, the search party rode out about two miles, though not far enough to discover the bodies of Elliott and his men, all killed by a large force of warriors who had emerged from camps downriver—camps whose existence was entirely unknown to Custer at the time of his initial attack. Benteen, who had been under Elliott's command, never let rest the accusation of "abandonment" of these men, a charge, in the minds of some, that called into question Custer's reputation as a military leader. Now nearly encircled by overwhelming numbers of warriors and with no help in sight, Reno not only must have questioned Custer's judgment but also may have wondered if he and his men had been abandoned.

Unnerved as he may have been by thoughts of Elliott's fate at the Washita, Reno's immediate concern was ammunition. Each soldier had carried into action one hundred rounds of carbine ammunition and twenty-four pistol cartridges, half on his person in loops and cartridge boxes on his waist belt and half in his saddlebag. They had been fighting furiously for nearly forty-five minutes. Often soldiers on a skirmish line laid out a row of cartridges on the ground beside them for quicker access when reloading. As the lines changed during the fighting, unused cartridges were lost in haste and remained unclaimed on the ground. In one way or another, the battalion was rapidly expending its cartridges. Sequestered and nearly surrounded, the major feared that the pack train with the ammunition mules might not reach his men until too late. It was time to break from the timber and head for higher, more defensible ground.

While Reno weighed his options and tactics, several officers and scouts around him pressed for an immediate decision. All of a sudden, what had been up until then a military discussion became personal and visceral: a bullet tore through the head of the scout known as Bloody Knife, who was mounted on his horse at the major's side, and his brains splattered directly onto Reno. Some believed that at that moment the major lost his composure; others perceived the coalescence of his thoughts in his thundering command, "Charge," which was overheard by Porter as he attended the wounded soldier.

Reno's intuition to abandon the temporary safety of the timber took the form of a wild scramble for horses and a massive, undisciplined ride through the trees onto the prairie and back across the Little Big Horn toward the hundred-foot-high bluffs beyond. The major rode at the head of the disarrayed soldiers, an officer putting his desperate plan into urgent motion, though also a negligent one in his disregard for organization and discipline, army tactics that safeguarded against the chaos of "every man for himself." For the soldiers not within earshot of Reno's shouted command, there was much delay in their departure. As the troopers became strung out along the route, it became easier for the Indians to pick them off one by one.

Porter's attention to the mortally wounded Klotzbucher did not go unnoticed by guide Charlie Reynolds. He reined in his horse long enough to lean down and warn the surgeon not to delay but to hurry out of the timber and up onto the bluffs along with the rest of the command. Porter heeded his advice, fumbling his medical equipment back into the saddlebags on his large horse, whose agitated behavior reflected the incessant noise of firearms at close range, dust, smoke, and a nearly palpable panic in the air. Just to get a boot into one stirrup seemed impossible as the black horse reared and resisted Porter's control. The doctor caught his breath: he was no longer among the protection of the soldiers, his horse was threatening to escape from him, and he was unarmed. His polite refusal of Reno's carbine now came back to haunt him. From then on, outright fright guided his actions: foot in stirrup, half in the saddle, then full seat with head lying low, grazing the horse's neck. Porter spurred his horse and barely hung on for the half-mile ride out onto the prairie and back toward the river, following soldiers ahead and even overtaking some along the way. In his blind haste Porter did not realize that he passed "Lonesome" Charlie Reynolds, dead on the ground, shot just minutes after he had warned the doctor back in the timber.[15]

The battalion was unable to reach the river at the point where it had crossed just about an hour earlier to begin the approach into the valley. Luckily, Major Reno found an equally fordable crossing where the Little Big Horn was only about twenty-five feet wide. The horses ahead had caved in the straight-cut bank, making an easier entrance into the water. But as they bunched up and slowed at this point, Porter wisely steered his horse a little to the left, where the bank was still sheer, and hardly slowed as he lunged into the river from five feet above. In late June the Little Big Horn ran high from winter runoff, and the water quickly rose to the edge of Porter's saddlebags. Horse and rider churned through the river toward the bank on the other side, which was higher, closer to eight feet. Again the momentum of the frantic riders slowed as they jockeyed to climb out of the channel. The ensuing snarl of men and horses presented the Indians on both sides of the river with easy targets. With no organized plan for the retreat or any defensive maneuvering, the soldiers were vulnerable to the same degrees of luck and misfortune. Porter's horse, as though sensing that speed counted for something, surged up the bank and pursued other cavalry mounts along a pony trail leading to the right and up a funnel-shaped ravine. The doctor now had but one concern: to hang on to his powerful horse as it labored up the steep clay hillside to the top of the bluff.[16]

At the top some soldiers dismounted, others simply fell from their saddles. All looked as though they wanted to keep on running. Lieutenant Varnum, hat in hand, berated the group: "For God's sake men, don't run, we have to go back and get our wounded men and officers!" Porter was not alone in feeling that they had been whipped. He approached Major Reno with his assessment: "Major, the men were pretty well demoralized, weren't they?" "No Sir," Reno sharply corrected him, "that was a charge." He knew that Reno had made a tough call in the timber, deciding to leave and run for higher ground, but now witnessed a man "a little embarrassed and flurried," who insisted on calling an uncoordinated retreat a charge. Having suffered the commander's retort, the doctor took his leave and made his way through clusters of spent horses and men in order to attend to numerous wounded soldiers. Many had been shot during the wild ride and had just managed to hang on to their horses until they reached the top of the bluff. They were the lucky ones. With the help of his orderly and some proper medical equipment, Porter set to treating the bullet wounds of the men around him. After the confusion of the retreat, it must have provided him a measure of relief to be able to get to work.[17]

With the arrival of each officer, soldier, and scout, reports of the fighting drifted from group to group. Porter's work did not prevent him from hearing DeWolf's name as soldiers told Major Reno of the surgeon's fate. No one could really explain why he had failed to follow the ravine to the right and instead had ascended a steep, narrow one to the left. Perhaps he had simply given rein to his horse, and the frightened animal veered to the nearer draw, trying to avoid the crowd of men and horses filing up the other one. The choice proved fatal: Indians waiting at the top shot and killed DeWolf outright; there was no way to retrieve his body at the time. Porter marked the death of his colleague and friend with a silent promise to recover the man's possessions and direct them to Fanny DeWolf.

Reno's battalion had been gathering on the hilltop for about ten minutes; it was just after 4:00 P.M. In all there were seven officers and eighty-four enlisted men. Forty officers, men, and scouts were unaccounted for: some still scrambling for safety in the dense underbrush near the river's edge, some dying, others already dead. Almost mysteriously, the Indians' relentless fire had abated. Although there were still sporadic shots coming up from the valley, the mass of warriors had ridden off. On the completely shadeless hilltop in the searing heat, the survivors now were arguably better able to defend themselves, but they were still wanting for ammunition and the aid of the nine other companies of the Seventh Cavalry. Exhaustion and dispirit seemed to preempt any attempts to move. As the officers debated Custer's whereabouts, at about 4:20 P.M. dust to the south turned their attention to the approach of Captain Benteen and his three companies. The mood of Reno's command lifted measurably. Help was on the way.

Captain Benteen had gone valley hunting as ordered, traveling some seven and a half miles in a two-hour period. Convinced that he would find nothing more and was tiring the horses needlessly, Benteen doubled back and rejoined the original trail at around 1:40 P.M. The pack train was just a half mile above him on the trail, making slow but steady progress toward the Little Big Horn Valley. The captain and his men watered their horses at a spot of low, soft, watery ground and then resumed the trail. While Reno had no communication from Custer after he was ordered to charge down the valley toward the Indian village, Benteen had received two messages: The first came with Sergeant Kanipe yelling about a big village ahead as he rode by carrying a message from Custer to Captain McDougall, commander of the pack-train escort. Shortly thereafter Trumpeter Martin appeared with what turned out to be the final message from Custer, written by Adjutant Cooke: "Benteen. Come on. Big village. Be quick, Bring packs. W. W. Cooke. P.S. Bring packs." Rather than turn around on the trail and try to hurry along the ammunition-bearing mules still behind him, Benteen chose to accelerate his own battalion toward the valley. At 4:10 P.M. he witnessed the tail end of Reno's retreat, with more Indians than even he had anticipated pursuing the soldiers.[18]

When Benteen finally arrived on the hilltop, his first consideration was the plight of Reno's battalion. The major lost no time in describing the timber fight, how Custer's promised support never materialized, and how the precarious ammunition supply had forced him to charge out of the valley for higher ground where he could see and be seen. Both officers wondered if Custer had continued along the bluffs parallel to the village, moving north and downstream, ultimately in the direction of General Terry's command. They had, in fact, heard some shooting from that direction. But Reno had insisted on waiting for the pack train to reach them in order to unload the ammunition and parcel it out to the soldiers. His order to sit tight confounded several officers, especially Captain Thomas Weir, whose own military instinct and sense of duty urged him to advance north toward the firing in search of Custer. But the chain of command held him in check.

Reno then organized a party of twelve men to help find one of the three fallen officers—Lieutenant Benjamin Hodgson—last seen badly wounded by the bluff-side riverbank. To search for the body of a single, presumably dead, man rather than ride to the possible aid of Custer and his entire battalion further dumbfounded some of the junior officers.[19] While the rescue group stole down a ravine to the river, where they found Hodgson's body, Porter left the wounded men under the watchful eye of Captain Myles Moylan and executed a brief search of his own.

He found the body of Doctor DeWolf in an adjacent ravine, bearing seven bullet holes: one in the abdomen and six in the head and face. For Porter, it was barely possible to connect this shot-up corpse with the fellow physician he had come to know, the man who had graduated from Harvard Medical School nearly one year earlier to the day. Porter searched his friend's pockets for personal possessions and his precious diary to send to his widow. He already knew that he would write to Fanny and reassure her that her husband had not been mutilated in any way: the living deserved to find some comforting detail in the otherwise dreadful news of a loved one's death.

Back on the hilltop, Captain Weir finally erupted with impatience and quite independently led his Company D north along the bluffs to a high point, searching for some sign of Custer and his men. Major

Reno still had not formulated a plan; in its absence Captain Benteen and other officers simply followed Weir out about a mile. Soldiers were straggling after the Weir-led party when Porter returned to the makeshift hospital area.

In his mad dash from the timber to the top of the bluffs, Reno had let slip more than proper military procedure—he had abandoned the wounded below. Now the major argued that his concern for the wounded soldiers gathered on the hilltop made him reluctant to move. The truth was that many of the thirteen men, injured in arms, legs, and torsos, could no longer ride. As difficult as it would be to follow Weir's lead, Reno finally acquiesced to the plan, and Porter and several officers began to arrange the transport of the wounded. It took four to six men to carry each of the five most seriously injured soldiers in blankets. Others served to lead the riderless horses. The cumbersome procession barely got underway when it became apparent that Weir, Benteen, and their men were returning in haste—and that they were being pursued. Urgently Captain Moylan, Lieutenant Mathey, and Doctor Porter began to arrange a place for the wounded. They wisely located the field hospital in a small depression in the center of the hilltop and encircled it with the horses and mules of the pack train, which had finally arrived shortly after 5:00 P.M. The injured soldiers were made as comfortable as possible on a tarpaulin spread on the sandy ground.

As the soldiers returned from their aborted search for Custer, they had very little time to establish a defense perimeter on the crests of the hilltop before an enormous body of Indians—many of whom had already fought Reno's command in the timbered area—threatened them from all sides. Packs, hardtack boxes, and saddles provided some protection for soldiers from the bullets coming at them from all directions, including high bluffs east of the breastworks. Even the hospital area was not safe. The terrible success of the Indians situated on the eastern bluff would earn it the name Sharpshooter Ridge.

Heavy fighting resumed around 6:30 P.M. and continued until dusk, closer to 9:00 P.M. The summer solstice and longest day of the year had occurred just four days earlier. The sun went down as a red ball, taking with it the ninety-degree heat. Evening could not come quickly enough for the cavalrymen; they needed the cover of darkness for defensive positioning and also believed that Indians would not fight at night. By the end of this second action on June 25, five other men had been killed and six more wounded. There were now nineteen patients in the field hospital. Together with Private Robinson and now Private Harry Abbotts, formerly assigned to Doctor DeWolf, Doctor Porter worked without relief as the sole surgeon responsible for the care of the seven companies—over 350 men—under siege on the hilltop.

Major Reno, Captain Benteen, and the other officers convened to assess the situation. The first fight—in the timber that afternoon and on the hilltop that evening—was thankfully over. Everything now had to be done to prepare for an inevitable assault to come in the morrow, undoubtedly an even more ferocious contest. By their count this would be the second battle, and indeed it was. Unknown to Reno, Benteen, and the others, the Seventh Cavalry also suffered a third fight in the Battle of the Little Big Horn.

Many hours earlier, as Reno's battalion approached the southern end of the village and as warriors rode out to confront him, women, children, and elders fled for safety north toward the lower end of the encampment near Medicine Tail Coulee and beyond. While Reno's men fought on the skirmish line and in the timber, Custer and his five companies traced the line of bluffs above the river, aiming squarely for the lower end of the village where those noncombatants had fled. As warriors fighting Reno learned of this advance, they abandoned Reno and sped northward to defend their families.

At least 1,500 warriors massed, many already primed for battle after confronting the soldiers in the timber. They rode well-nourished, rested ponies to confront Custer's column of just over 200 men riding trail-weary mounts. The Indians knew the terrain, a topography that the lieutenant colonel was barely grasping. For Custer and the U.S. Army, this battle against these "hostiles" was all about westward expansion across the northern plains, the right to prospect for gold in the Black Hills, and the drive to "civilize" the Indians. The response of the Sioux and Northern Cheyenne derived from more fundamental needs and desires: the immediate protection and safety of families and the very survival of their culture and way of life. On that day the warriors' temperament was defiant and their purpose uncompromising.

Reno's battalion, fortifying on the hilltop, had already confronted this fact. Still, not a man there on the night of June 25 had any idea that the decisive engagement of the Battle of the Little Big Horn already had taken place. Just four miles north of their position, under the cover of an indifferent darkness, Custer and all of his 210 men lay dead.[20]

6

A True Field Hospital

THE DIGGING, SCRATCHING, AND CLAWING got underway almost immediately. Short on proper tools, soldiers obeyed Major Reno's orders to carve out protective rifle pits by using butcher knives, table forks, tins cups, and meat-can halves.[1] Sun-baked and hardened, the soil barely chipped apart. Most hoped, like Lieutenant Edward Godfrey, that a spindly sagebrush might help deflect a bullet. Even the slightest depression in the ground offered comfort. Fear and urgency overruled hunger and exhaustion, and the men scraped for hours in the darkness.

As the shooting subsided and the attackers withdrew to their village nearly two miles away, Reno, Captain Benteen, and the other officers realized that they had only a few hours under the cover of darkness to adjust and strengthen their defensive position around the perimeter of the hilltop. The first command to dig rifle pits was followed by "Build breastworks," and soon soldiers amassed what they could of saddles, packs, boxes of hardtack, sacks of beans, sacks of corn and oats, and blankets in front of their sculpted depressions.[2] Nothing was left unused: even horses killed during the evening fight were dragged from the corral, their bodies fitted into the breastworks and, where possible, covered with some dirt. Gradually the perimeter gained shape, affording the soldiers a measure of security, albeit false since a bullet could easily penetrate any single item in the patchwork barricade—even a dead horse.

Reno and Benteen were fully aware that the Indians still watched them and were positioned not only to block easy access to the water in the river below but also to prevent the cavalry from stealing off in the night. The officers agreed to keep the men busy building the defenses and allow them some sleep; both activities might distract them from their relentless thirst and any apprehension of what was to come. The command would be ready by dawn. Benteen ordered a bugler prepared to sound reveille at two in the morning, not only to awaken any sleeping soldiers but also to tell the Indians that the Seventh Cavalry was ready.

At the core of the hilltop, sequestered from the peripheral activity, Acting Assistant Surgeon Porter commanded his own clutch of soldiers: two orderlies and nineteen wounded men. Thirteen troopers had wounds from the timber fight, the retreat, or the frantic climb up the bluffs. Six others had been shot during the evening combat. Soldiers and Indian scouts lay side by side. They were of various ranks, belonging to different companies, even to different tribes. Only the severity of their wounds distinguished them here.

Most lay under an officer's shelter half, each suspended very low and secured with the few items at hand, largely hardtack boxes and packs.[3] Porter felt sincerely grateful to Lieutenant Mathey for his hurried construction of the field hospital, situated in an irregularly shaped basin of possibly 1,000 square feet, providing limited space for the many supine patients and barely enough room for the surgeon and his orderlies to maneuver and minister. Adding to the spatial density was the mass of perhaps 450 to 500 animals—all of the remaining cavalry horses and the 140 mules from the pack train—that nearly encircled the hospital. In the darkness Porter could hear the animals breathing and shifting along the picket lines. Packers had finally freed them of their saddles and packs but could not relieve them of their severe thirst and hunger. Porter understood perfectly well the screen these animals were meant to provide from the Indians' rifle fire.

The surgeon was restricted in what he could do for his patients during the moonless night. Afraid that a fire might attract a sniper's shot, Porter resorted to care by touch alone. He continued to follow his cardinal guidelines—stop the bleeding, ease the pain—but without light he could barely remove debris from the wounds or tie off any severed blood vessels. The various injuries to arms, hands, wrists, knees, and ankles needed field dressings and even redressings. Here and there Porter faced an even more daunting restriction: he lacked the volume of water necessary to wash away the blood, clots, and debris in the wounds and soak the lint for cold-water dressings. His only option was to wring the ample blood out of a soaked bandage, dust the wound with pain-reducing powdered morphine sulfate, and simply reapply the old bandage.[4] It was hardly his standard of care.

The lack of water hampered more than attending to wounds. Porter's patients groaned from their insistent thirst. Reno's men had managed to drink very briefly from the Little Big Horn before they started the accelerated charge toward the village in the midafternoon. Even then they were thirsty, some having been deprived of early morning coffee because of the haste of the advance. The ninety-degree heat of the day, coupled with battle exertion, had left all the cavalrymen severely thirsty and dehydrated. But the thirst of the wounded men was amplified by their blood loss: they simply had less liquid volume in their bodies. It was understandable, then, when Private Julius Helmer, originally from Hanover, Germany, cried out loudly for a drink. Shot through the bowels, his fate swung between hemorrhaging to death from internal bleeding or dying from infection and peritonitis, or abdominal inflammation. Porter's experience resigned him to the man's imminent death, but the doctor still suffered from his inability to give him the simple comfort of a drink of water. Helmer died that evening.

While serving under General Crook in Arizona Territory, Porter had reflected on the difficulties of becoming a practicing physician.

Those desert conditions and life on the march, which had seemed so arduous at the time, now paled grossly in comparison with his current predicament. James DeWolf was dead; the care of more than 350 men, including the 19 already wounded, belonged to Porter alone. He could instruct the few soldiers detailed to hospital duty in basic medical techniques: such knowledge would be a vast improvement over what little the soldiers understood about first aid, including their belief that spitting tobacco juice into a wound would prevent infection. The doctor could rely on his own good medical training, cool head, steady hand, and youthful stamina to address his patients' physical demands. But he was less sure about how to contend with their emotional duress. The frightful night sponsored some dark thoughts even in Porter's mind. He felt that there was "no prospect of relief" and expected "every moment to be murdered, and, perhaps, tortured and burned." His "command"— the wounded—was indeed physically protected, first by a circle of animal mass, then by a perimeter of Seventh Cavalry troopers. Moreover, despite their physical isolation on a godforsaken hilltop in eastern Montana, everyone assumed that battalions of cavalry and companies of infantry under Custer, General Terry, and Colonel Gibbon were heading toward them according to plan.[5]

Despite these reassuring thoughts, Porter continued to ruminate on the plight of those in his charge. He was their caretaker and would administer to their needs at all cost. Therein lay both his military duty and his physician's oath. But his efforts could never make up for the incapacitation and immobility of the wounded. He was not alone in this realization. Every man in that makeshift hospital knew how dependent he was on his comrades fortifying the hilltop perimeter. Yet Reno's horsemen also remembered the great number of fellow soldiers—nearly one-fourth of the original battalion—left behind to an unimaginable fate in the timber, at the river crossing, or on the slopes of the bluffs, all sacrificed to the hasty and ill-coordinated "charge" led by the major. During the nighttime hours, they became further unnerved by a rumor circulating of a plan to steal away from the hilltop along the back trail that Benteen and the pack train had followed to reach them. An essential element of the rumored plan—to abandon the immobile wounded—stunned all in the hospital and aggravated the general sense of helplessness.[6] The thought of dying on a besieged hilltop gnawed at most, but the added prospect of physical torture at the hands of the Indians created a mental horror that compounded the pain from wounds or ache from thirst. The only available means of escape—a pistol kept close at hand—gave men a semblance of control. They would feel no sense of cowardice or shame in saving the last bullets for themselves.

The feelings of dread shared by all in the hospital came to an abrupt end when a cavalry bugler sounded reveille. At that point it was too late to abandon anyone, and for that the wounded could feel some relief. But the fight ahead and the real possibility of being overrun by what most judged to be many thousands of warriors kept everyone on edge. The crack of two shots ushered in June 26 and yet another fight in the Battle of the Little Big Horn. It was barely half past two in the morning. There was no more time for reflection, hardly even a moment for fear.

The firing, fierce from the start, grew hotter with increasing daylight. Indians shot from below and from the higher points surrounding the dug-in battalion. Bullets flew in at various angles, hitting men even in their sides and backsides as they lay in their shallow rifle pits. Casualties increased, and some never made it to the field hospital. Private Julien Jones rolled onto his back to take off the overcoat he had worn against the night chill and was shot in the heart. When Captain French's horse was shot in the head and began staggering precariously in the corral, Private Henry Voight rushed to lead it out, at which point he too was shot in the head.

Others reached the hospital, to no avail. Private George Lell of Company H, under Benteen's capable command, had only just elevated himself to shoot when he was hit in the stomach. He folded and fell to the ground. Fellow soldiers Jacob Adams and Charles Windolph carried the human bundle to the hospital, where Porter mentally triaged him into the category of mortally wounded. One glance at how the bullet had ripped apart the soldier's abdomen told the surgeon all he needed to know about Lell's fate. As the man bled, his thirst grew, and he begged for water. The drink eventually ran out of his wound.[7] Lell realized his final lot, and before he died he asked to be raised up to see his fellow cavalrymen in action.

It was not an easy thing to watch a man die. While Lell conducted his own last minutes with some composure and dignity, Private Andrew Moore, among others, could hardly endure the pain from the bullet wound through his back and into his stomach and kidney. Moore no sooner arrived in the hospital than he begged Porter for something to ease the pain. A dose of laudanum helped quiet not only the man but also those immediately nearby who were agitated by Moore's audible suffering—they could not help but imagine their own fates mirrored in such deaths.[8]

The sight of any penetrating wound to the abdomen left Doctor Porter disheartened and resigned. In general, surgeons still shied away from performing operations in the large cavities like the thorax and upper or lower abdomen. Even if efforts to staunch the internal bleeding succeeded, it was nearly guaranteed that infection and peritonitis would follow if a projectile had perforated the intestinal tract. Death was almost inevitable. Indeed, one by one, the soldiers with such penetrating wounds died. In contrast, Private Francis Reeves, a patient in this category, seemed to defy the odds. He had been shot in the front of his belt while riding out of the timber on the previous day; a second bullet had torn through his thigh. Upon examination, Porter discovered the miraculous path of the first bullet, sparing Reeves's backbone by barely an inch because it had been deflected, most likely by the belt. Porter considered him an "abdominal penetration" patient, but the wound was less messy and, with luck, much less destructive internally. He cleansed the wound with a carbolic-acid solution, the antiseptic approach that had already won Scotland's Doctor Joseph Lister a reputation for successful—and infection-free—surgeries. Reeves was decidedly uncomfortable but not looking too pale, and Porter could entertain private hopes for his survival.[9]

Most of the other injured soldiers in the hospital had flesh or perforating wounds, where the bullet had an entrance and an exit. Bright daylight aided Porter in examining the injuries, exploring with a long silver probe, or often with just his finger, to find the projectile and whatever debris had been dragged in along its path. Surgeons debrided wounds of all sorts of foreign matter: shreds of clothing, bits of leather from boots and pouches, and pocket items such as coins, keys, and watches. Once he removed any such material and perhaps the bullet too, Porter or his orderlies cleansed the wound with a sponge and the little water they reserved and then applied a field dressing, "two layers of lint saturated in cold water, topped with a piece of oiled silk, all held in place by a pocket handkerchief" or a rag. Where the injury was especially painful, the attendant added some tincture of opium to the first layer of lint. The dressing was both absorbent and protective, loosely packed to permit drainage of the suppuration, or pus.[10]

In a surgeon's ideal world, all wounds healed "by first intention"—that is, with bulges or granules gradually forming on the surface, unimpeded in the process by the formation of any pus. This was rarely the case, however, because the process of debridement often failed to remove all debris, or the surgeon's probe or finger introduced microscopic foreign matter into the wound. Thus it was almost expected that pus would form and drain from a wound, but the type of pus remained unpredictable. If thick, yellow, less foul smelling, and local, surgeons called it "laudable" and felt confident about the patient's recovery. When the pus was thinner in consistency, tinged with blood, and foul smelling from putrefying tissue, it was termed "malignant," and for good reason, for it signaled an infection that killed tissue, would spread beyond the wound site, and was most often life threatening.[11]

In 1846, when anesthesia—both ether and chloroform—first came into use, surgery gained the element of time necessary for longer operations.[12] Patients experienced an unprecedented level of comfort by not feeling the pain of surgery. With a solid understanding of human anatomy and the ability to control hemorrhage, surgeons attempted more-complex procedures nearly everywhere in the body. Technical success increasingly rewarded the surgeon, and the profession began to shed its former "crude" reputation. Trained physicians, like Henry Porter, demonstrated confidence in their technical skills and control of various procedures. What they could not control, however, and what all too often still undermined all their technical success, was postoperative infection.

American physicians and the general public in 1876 still believed that putrid air and decaying vegetable and animal matter constituted the "miasmas" that *caused* infection and disease. These "bad airs" were considered the agents that gave rise to the pus in wounds. Cleanliness and proper hygiene were strong public priorities of the time, endorsed as the primary disease-fighting weapons. Few physicians, however, had any real scientific understanding of the precise cause of infection and cross-infection. Not until Joseph Lister in Scotland and Robert Koch in Germany proved the existence of germs and microbes would surgeons finally gain insight into the process of infection as well as grasp the insidious role they themselves had long played in both patient health and demise: those who intended to heal often also unwittingly infected. With the formal advent of germ theory and, consequently, antisepsis during the 1870s and 1880s, surgery gained the next level of control, and the technical success of the surgical procedure was followed more often by healthy postoperative recovery. Laudable pus, no longer believed to be the derivative of atmospheric "miasmas" and anticipated as part of the routine healing process, was almost banished by the use of carbolic acid and other antiseptic materials used routinely during operations.

By 1876 the European medical profession was on the cusp of understanding how and why so many patients died after seemingly successful surgeries. Within years scientists would see "germs" under the microscope and identify them as "causative" agents of infection. The realization would quickly usher in antiseptic surgery and the field of microbiology. But on that day in late June 1876, Henry Porter had no need for a germ theory to explain why his patients were suffering. It was so elemental. As far as he was concerned, the Indians need not shoot another single bullet. Just save their ammunition and sit tight around the entrenchments and prevent all access to the glistening water in the Little Big Horn River below. Eventually the corralled cavalry would simply die of thirst and dehydration. The bleeding men in the field hospital would be the first to go.

Against his better judgment but out of desperation, Porter had given a small amount of medicinal whiskey to each of the patients. Sergeant Charles Weihe, although badly injured in the right elbow, treated each of the wounded to a spoonful of precious jelly from a jar he had carried along in his saddlebag. Pieces of prickly pear cactus, the lead of bullets, and small pebbles failed to stimulate much saliva in their mouths. With throats so parched and sore, tongues stuck like thick wads of cotton against the cheeks and teeth, and lips stiffened and cracked. Few could close their mouths let alone utter any comprehensible words.[13]

Doctor Porter listened to their heartrending groans and studied their field dressings, which were hardly absorbent and protective. He was failing these men as a physician. It was time to alert a commanding officer of the dire conditions in the hospital. Although Major Reno was the ranking officer, many sensed that he had lost his self-control, and they turned instead to Captain Benteen, inspired by his coolness and bravery. Word of the desperate need for water from Porter reached the captain out on the perimeter. He had already witnessed one man go insane from thirst and be tied up fast by his comrades. No need to invite any more of that kind of drama: there was already stress enough from the steady firing all around. Benteen conferred with other officers, and they announced their willingness to let men volunteer to create a water party.

Of the nineteen soldiers who came forward, the officers allowed a dozen to descend to the river. With two canteens per man and six two-gallon camp kettles, the party scrambled the one hundred exposed yards to get to the head of the ravine. From there they were concealed in the ravine all the way from the bluff to the base, but they had to dash across nearly twenty open yards to the river. While cavalry sharpshooters occupied the Indians on the opposite bank of the river, the volunteers filled the canteens and buckets and made it back to the hilltop without injury. They dispersed the water among the wounded and other soldiers but provided an allotment so meager that most men punctuated their brief enjoyment with a hearty curse. Porter relished the relief given to his patients by these small sips but remained helpless to wash and dress their wounds properly.

As gunshot injuries multiplied, the hospital population continued to swell, and casualties lay ever closer to the corral of horses and mules. Initially, officers had assigned soldiers to tend these animals. When a horse was killed, the men rolled it on its back and tied the other horses to the legs of the dead one. This happened often enough to free up the handlers and release them back to their companies fighting on the perimeter. Bullets and arrows were not the only weapons in this battle. Along with thirst, the Indians also added immobility to their arsenal: depriving the cavalry of its valuable horses diminished the prospects for escape. This was not an original strategy. In their attacks on Indian villages, soldiers regularly targeted the pony herds in their persistent effort to force the bands onto the reservations. A quick death was the kindest, but more often the animals suffered terrible wounds and became agitated. The situation was not without consequence for the wounded men sitting and lying very nearby. All risked being further injured or crushed outright by a thousand-pound animal thrashing around in the throes of death or setting off a panic among the rest. Without the holders to control them, horses and mules became one more imminent threat to the wounded. Working painstakingly among his patients, Porter too remained aware of the corral activity, apprehensive about animals falling on his patients and fearful of what he had assumed from the beginning: that the Indians would shoot into and through the horses and eventually hit the men beyond. Although it brought some relief when soldiers dragged the dead animals out to the breastworks and thereby eased the dangerous crowding so close to the hospital, the culling only left the wounded further exposed to Indian fire.

On the perimeter, scout George Herendeen took aim from behind his dead horse, which had been lying long enough to become bloated with gas that released with a hiss each time a bullet thudded into the carcass.[14] Exposed in the hot sun, the dead and dying animals produced a nearly unbearable stench, a miasma of profound disease-producing capability, according to the contemporary medical belief. That the awful smell had to compete with more-acute threats was oddly fortunate because the stench receded into the general atmosphere permeated with smoke, sweat, and blood.

The cry for water reached a critical pitch again early in the afternoon. The patients wanted to slake their dogged thirst, and Porter and the orderlies needed to moisten the cold-water dressings covering the more serious wounds. Every soldier on the skirmish line wanted relief from the gunsmoke and dust-filled air that choked and nearly blinded them. Volunteers organized for a second water party and followed the same trail and tactics used by the first group. As they stole down the steep ravine, four of the cavalry's best sharpshooters busied the Indians close to the river with some careful but rapid firing. They provided the cover necessary for the water bearers to scramble to the river, fill canteens and kettles, and return to relative safety in the earthen folds of the ravine. At nearly six feet, Private Mike Madden was just about the tallest trooper in the regiment and certainly the tallest among the volunteers in this water party. An ample target, he nonetheless took his chances in a dash to the river and what proved to be a nearly successful return. Stealing back to the ravine, the soldier teamed with Madden to carry the full kettle felt his partner drop his side of the container but continued to drag it to safety. As he did two other soldiers lurched out of hiding to pull an obviously injured Madden into shelter. The luck of the water parties had run out: a bullet had shattered Madden's right leg above the ankle. He protested any rescue, not wanting to endanger the lives of others, but his comrades knew of only one humane option, and that was to haul the burly Irishman back up the ravine to the hospital. Porter would not have considered the mangled limb exactly a fair price for the water suddenly at hand. Up to that point he had explored for bullets and debrided numerous wounds, removed bits of bone from a shattered cheek, and extracted four teeth from the mouth of another with a similar injury.[15] The penetrating abdominal wounds had been left to nature.

Serving in Arizona under Crook had well prepared Porter to remove arrows using an extracting device designed in 1862 by Doctor J. H. Bill, assistant surgeon, U.S. Army: Widen the wound just enough to slide the wire-loop device down next to the shaft of the arrow, direct the wire loop over the tip of the arrowhead, snare it, and then very carefully withdraw the entire arrow. The sooner it was properly removed, the less likely bodily fluids would loosen and separate the animal tendons binding the arrowhead to the shaft. Above all, surgeons instructed soldiers, never just yank out the shaft since the odds of leaving behind the sharp, sometimes barbed arrowhead were nearly 100 percent.[16] Despite this excellent preparation, Porter strangely had yet to address an arrow wound in this battle. The Sioux and Cheyenne warriors were well armed with rifles and carbines, and any cut down of a wound was done to extract a bullet.

Arrowhead removal ranked among the most difficult operations for a military surgeon, but it still held second place to amputation. It was midafternoon when soldiers delivered Privates James Wilber Darcy and Mike Madden to the hospital, both casualties of the water party. Each was wounded in the lower leg, but there was a profound difference between the two injuries. Darcy had fractured his tibia, and Porter splinted the leg from the knee to the foot. This was standard and effective treatment for a simple fracture. Madden's injury was a compound fracture, where broken bones near the ankle had torn through the skin, and the wound had become an entrance point for all agents of infection. To limit the progress and extent of infection in Madden's body, Porter realized that he would have to undertake "the ultimate form of debridement" by amputating the leg—it was the only way to save the private's life. He knew that timing was critical in order to limit the spread of infection and exploit the man's still courageous frame of mind and strong physical condition. Waiting to amputate chanced the patient losing physical health to infection and the debilitating dread of the operation.[17]

Porter's readiness to amputate Madden's lower right leg was suddenly compromised by a turn of events in the battle. Officers and soldiers fighting on the hilltop perimeter had been perplexed for some time during the afternoon by the steady decrease in shooting from the Indians. Then heavy smoke began drifting across the Little Big Horn. The Indians had set fire to the grass, and the smoke screened the valley. The cavalry studied the bottomland carefully, expecting at any moment a sudden, renewed attack by the warriors. But as the drifting smoke thinned and separated into discrete billows, they glimpsed an entirely unexpected sight. Indians on horseback and on foot—a mass possibly a mile wide and several miles long—were moving southward with travois, dogs, and their immense pony herd. Private Charles Windolph likened the vision to a "Biblical exodus; the Israelites moving into Egypt; a mighty tribe on the march."[18] Before them they saw the spectacle of as many as seven thousand Indians moving as a well-organized and coordinated body out of the Little Big Horn Valley. The men on the hilltop realized that they had come against and fought more warriors in the previous thirty-six hours than any cavalryman had ever before seen amassed.

Suspecting some form of trickery, the men waited in their rifle pits and trenches. Henry Porter delayed the amputation, thinking that "the Indians were up to some bloodier mischief," until the oblique light of the late afternoon finally dictated that he wait and operate in the broad daylight the next day.[19] He had plenty to do before then, now that he had water at hand and fifty-nine wounded soldiers in the hospital. It had been nearly forty-eight hours since Porter had last slept. With the departure of the Indians, the number of wounded in the hospital might at long last stabilize, allowing the doctor and the orderlies to catch up on caretaking and perhaps get their own rest.

Major Reno, still the senior officer present, gave a series of commands for duties to be performed in the lull. While designated guards kept watch, other soldiers led many of the horses and mules down the ravines to the river that they could only smell but not taste for the previous twenty-four hours. The wounded animals were watered on their picket lines on the hilltop. Soldiers gathered the bodies of their dead comrades from the field hospital and along the periphery of the defense perimeter and, in the words of Private Windolph, "gently buried [them] in the shallow trenches [they] had dug for the living." Pieces of hardtack boxes supplied headboards for some of the graves. Reno then ordered the entire camp to shift closer to the river and as far away as possible from the overwhelming stench of the many dead horses and mules. Lastly, cooks built fires to make hot coffee, fry bacon, and soak hardtack in the grease, a kindly gesture to make the three-by-three-inch square flour biscuits—nicknamed "old fire bricks," "teeth dullers," "sheet iron crackers," and "worm castles"—more palatable. For many, this was their first meal in thirty-six hours. Guards rotated on duty throughout the night, but the rest of the men succumbed to exhaustion and fitful sleep.[20]

Acting Assistant Surgeon Porter ended his second day in charge of a field hospital serving fifty-nine soldiers whose wounds ranged from slight to severe and mortal. He had witnessed intimately the results of the "Expedition against hostile Sioux," and while his mood did not favor the Indians, neither did it sympathize with the U.S. government. The loss of men's lives and the diminution of the quality of the lives of others as a result of injury sparked in him a vengeful "hope to punish the red devils, whom the government and Indian department have so splendidly armed with improved rifles to kill United States troops." Taking stock of the situation, the weary surgeon dismissed all military analysis in favor of a forthright judgment: "what a bloody, sickening, disastrous fight." In hindsight, while the government's role in creating the mess was not lost on Porter, the self-inflicted horror of the hilltop fight was even worse than the surgeon realized. The Indians had used not only the rifles supplied to them over the years by the government to hunt buffalo, but also the carbines they had captured when they annihilated Custer's battalion the previous day. Seventh Cavalry weapons and bullets had wounded, maimed, and killed Seventh Cavalry soldiers.[21]

Never Leave the Wounded Behind

"THE GOVERNMENT PAYS YOU TO GET SHOT AT." Enlisted soldiers had heard Captain Benteen's words all too often. During roll call on the morning of June 27, however, his blunt statement took on a dreadful resonance. So many silences punctuated the orderly call of names in each company, it seemed as if the larger silence of the vast western space around the troopers had infiltrated their fragile presence on that exposed hilltop. Benteen surveyed the scene and flatly concluded, "We are abandoned to our fate."[1]

Despite the bright sunlit morning and startling absence of Indians anywhere around, most of the men remained on guard, convinced that Indian wile was at work not far away. They tried to scrutinize the ravines and valley below, but with tired eyes still smarting from carbine smoke and the gigantic grass fire set to conceal the village's departure the previous late afternoon, it was difficult to discern many details in the landscape. What did catch their attention at midmorning was not activity but its byproduct: a large dust cloud about five miles away to the north and approaching down the Little Big Horn Valley. All eyes strained to overcome their weariness in the desire to know the source of that cloud.

Already soldiers had worked long hours in the early morning to improve the hilltop living conditions. Major Reno had ordered the camp shifted onto the bench of land above the water carriers' ravine, affording closer access to the river below. More importantly, perhaps, it partially relieved those still alive of the overwhelming stench of death. As soon as the officers judged it safe, care was taken to bury the dead soldiers as best as possible. Privates James Tanner and Henry Voight shared a final resting place in a shallow rifle pit, their names etched in lead pencil on a piece of box fashioned as a headboard.[2]

Thwarted in an earlier attempt on the late afternoon of June 25 to recover the body of 2nd Lieutenant Benjamin Hodgson, Major Reno now wasted no time in dispatching four soldiers to locate the remains of the well-liked officer. Others, including Henry Porter, set out to retrieve the body of Doctor DeWolf. Soldiers carried the stiffened forms supported across pairs of carbines to the hilltop. DeWolf received a careful burial, covered with enough well-packed dirt to protect against coyotes and other ravenous animals. Lieutenant Hodgson earned the consideration of being wrapped in an army blanket and placed in a properly dug grave. Army rank served in death as in life.[3]

The dust cloud in the distance brought an abrupt halt to activity on the hilltop. Buglers sounded assembly, and soldiers hurried to corral the horses and mules in a protected area, preparing for the possible renewal of fighting. Not to be left high and dry again, the men filled every possible vessel—quart canteens and camp kettles—with water and lugged the liquid treasure to their position. Then they settled in for an hour of suspense, still unable to discern whether friend or foe was the source of the rolling cloud.[4]

Porter remained appreciative of all considerations afforded the wounded. The relocated field hospital now consisted of a few shelter tents, under which lay the most seriously wounded, while others with lesser injuries found shade along the edges of the tents and even in the shadows cast by the horses and mules still corralled very close by. Porter addressed routine patient care, using the available water to reapply cold-water dressings to the various wounds. The lint material and loose bandages allowed critical drainage of pus while also preventing dirt, flies, and noxious vapors from entering. And there were still plenty of vapors. The human dead had been buried, but the animal dead—almost fifty horses and mules—littered the hilltop. Stiffened legs thrust straight out of bloated, gas-filled bodies, and the nauseating stench of rotting flesh—the smell of cadaverine—seemed to crown the entire area. The odor attracted flies; the corpses already hosted maggots which produced yet more flies. It was a deadly cycle. Major Reno had smartly moved the entire camp away from the physical pestilence; nonetheless, the flies and odors pursued the wounded and the healthy alike.

Surgeon Porter was gravely concerned about the foul smell. In his mind it was not simply offensive, it was an invisible menace. In medical school he had read enough in *System of Surgery* by Doctor Samuel D. Gross to respect what the eminent surgeon identified as the "toxic effects of the tainted atmosphere."[5] Gross argued that such noxious air transported invisible disease and infection-causing toxins, the source of pus in the wounds. No one was immune to the effects, but the sickly and injured were more generally susceptible. In Porter's medical opinion, his patients, and the rest of the cavalry-men for that matter, were at risk as much from the unseen threat of the hilltop miasma as they were from the still unidentified party approaching down the valley.

Keen vision among officers and soldiers finally revealed that the dust resulted not from Indian trickery but from approaching cavalry. Feelings of relief and even excitement began to slacken taut muscles. Chatter broke the ominous silence as men voiced speculations about the identity of the approaching force—perhaps Custer's promised support would now arrive. The lieutenant colonel was certainly tardy, but Reno's men could forgive the delay. Gradually they noticed a critical detail about the approaching horses. Each of the twelve companies in the Seventh Cavalry, except one, had been assigned a uniform horse color: Company A—dark bay; C, K—sorrel; B, F, H, I, L, M—light bays; D—black; E—gray; G—mixed colors;

Trumpeters—gray. The color scheme served organizationally on the battlefield and was even more impressive when the Seventh Cavalry marched together. Custer had ridden off on June 25 with five companies: C, E, F, I, and L. When the soldiers on the hilltop could not find a gray-horse company among the ones riding up the valley, they realized that it could not be Custer and his battalion drawing near. Reno and his men also reasoned that the approaching column probably could not be General Terry with Colonel Gibbon's Montana column since Custer would now have been with them. But few in the battalion allowed such details to interfere with their celebration of imminent rescue. Men cheered and hollered; buglers blurted calls without realizing that the wind carried their martial airs away from the approaching force.[6]

As it happened, the dust cloud signaled the arrival of Terry and Gibbon's column, made up of the Second Cavalry and the Seventh Infantry. The troops had begun the last day of their planned march to meet up with Custer that morning from a camp just nine miles away. Their approach had become known to Reno and his men only within a five-mile distance; however, the Terry-Gibbon column had unwittingly been aiding the embattled battalion for over eighteen hours. By midafternoon on the previous day, Indian scouts from the village had spied this column moving up the Little Big Horn Valley toward their position. The Indians' own casualties from the fights with Reno in the timber, with Custer, and then again with Reno on the hilltop, as well as their dwindling supply of ammunition, persuaded them to avoid yet another battle—so costly in manpower and materiel—and simply move on. When the warriors encircling Reno's hill ceased firing so abruptly around 3:00 P.M. on June 26, the major and Captain Benteen assumed their enemy had resorted to some devious plan. Little did they know that their salvation was so near at hand, even though it would be another twenty hours before they were united with the Montana column.

The scene in the Little Big Horn Valley perplexed General Terry and Colonel Gibbon. Their advance had led them straight through the abandoned Indian encampment. Nearing the end of the village—a black and smoking landscape—they suddenly came upon dead cavalry horses and the bodies of soldiers spread over the area toward the hilltop. Terry and Gibbon's confusion at the sight of these abandoned casualties could hardly compare with the shock they received when 1st Lieutenant James H. Bradley, chief of scouts for the Seventh Infantry, finally caught up with the two senior commanders. On Gibbon's orders, Bradley had explored the area east of the village. He now related his unimaginable discovery: Custer and the men in his battalion were all dead, their corpses naked, bloated, and blistering in the sunlight in the adjacent ravines and coulees and on the eastern hillsides. For the officers listening to Bradley, their initial sense of disbelief slowly gave way to a feeling of profound grief. But the 200 or so bodies found by the scout, combined with about 40 more in the area around the column, still failed to account for the entire Seventh Cavalry. Only when Gibbon began to study more intently what he initially thought to be animals or cedar trees up on the bluffs to his left did he realize that these were men, perhaps the remaining troopers.

At the meeting of General Terry and Major Reno on the hilltop, military formality was mixed with tearful greetings, joy traded with sadness. The picture of the last three days began to take shape for both officers. In his style of quiet command, Terry ordered his staff to organize the relief of these survivors, beginning with the transport of all the wounded to the comfort and safety of the bivouac Gibbon's men were preparing in the cooler timber by the river. Doctor John Williams, chief medical officer for the entire campaign, had accompanied the general to Reno's camp and now offered his medical services. An exhausted Henry Porter realized that his patients finally would be relieved of the heat and exposure, the pestilence and its vapors.

Gibbon also turned his full attention to the welfare of the wounded. "In savage warfare to leave one's wounded behind is out of the question," he emphasized.[7] In the timber area soldiers followed the colonel's orders, precisely setting up camp, finding grass for the horses, and clearing the area of "offensive" dead horses and bodies, the latter respectfully buried. On the hilltop Gibbon contributed manpower to make litters of blankets and old canvas stretched across abandoned tipi poles. Finally, he assigned his lone surgeon to help Porter with the care of his more than fifty patients.

Twenty-four-year-old assistant surgeon Holmes Offley Paulding, a first lieutenant, the post surgeon at Fort Ellis, and the sole medical officer in the Montana column, must have been quietly stunned by the sight of the field hospital. He surveyed the sheer number of wounded men under Porter's able care. Despite the desperate conditions, Paulding perhaps envied his colleague's experience on the hilltop. Gibbon's command had somehow avoided direct contact with the Indians since the column departed from Fort Ellis on March 30. As a result Paulding had suffered only the simple monotony of the journey. On May 1 he confessed in a letter to his mother, "I wish we would go somewhere away from here instead of purposelessly fooling around in sagebrush bottoms all summer." He also criticized Gibbon's passive, by-the-book style of command, which seemed to preclude any action or adventure: "This whole trip has been a miserable farce and everything has been as disagreeable as idiotic, pig-headed stupidity could make it." In his personal diary Paulding flatly concluded, "If I am to be under the command of such imbecile damned fools, I think I will get out of it as soon as possible."[8]

Paulding may have felt cheated. After graduating from George Washington University Medical School in 1874, he was soon thereafter one of the very few young doctors to take and pass the army's rigorous medical exam, becoming a commissioned officer in the medical corps. Luck stayed with him when he was assigned to the Department of Dakota, serving first at Fort Snelling, Minnesota, and then in 1875 at Fort Abraham Lincoln, the new home of Custer and the Seventh Cavalry. Paulding socialized with the lieutenant colonel and other officers, including his colleague in surgery Doctor George Lord. Yet when the army transferred him to Fort Ellis, Montana Territory, in October 1875, Paulding did not at first realize the huge step he had taken away from the center of action. It became increasingly apparent, however, during the march with the Montana column, and it was shockingly apparent on June 27 as he stood in the field hospital and fathomed what Henry Porter must have experienced serving with the Seventh Cavalry. Paulding could hold no personal resentment toward Porter, and perhaps he envied what the contract surgeon had accomplished in almost thirty-six hours on that hilltop. Only he and Doctor Williams could understand the feat of sheer stamina this lone surgeon had achieved.

Paulding had written to his mother on April 24 of his anger about being the only medical officer for the roughly 450 men of the Montana column: "I would rather be shot than have any of the men so injured as to require operations impossible of performance by one *unassisted* surgeon, for I can't conceive of anything worse than to know what should be done for a man and not be able to do it."[9] In fact, his nightmare had been Porter's reality for over two days. The contract surgeon had attended to wounds and dressings and performed operations with little time to question his role or capabilities. Paulding acknowledged that Porter had more than succeeded in a situation where he himself might well have failed. Excluding the few who had died under Porter's care—all from abdominal wounds—his patients by degrees were surviving. And the surgeon was still at work, readying each of the wounded for transport to Gibbon's camp in the valley. Porter had performed admirably, perhaps to the surprise of the young assistant surgeon and to the satisfaction of Surgeon Williams.

As difficult as it had been to scale the bluffs on the afternoon of June 25, it was for some of these same soldiers even more perilous, two days later, to descend to the river and timbered area below. Four to six men supported each tipi-pole litter or clutched the edges of each blanket sling. The steep hillside pitch challenged the sure footing of the carriers, constantly interrupting their attempt at group coordination. The wounded man on the litter or in the blanket sling suffered a continuous jostling and feared that a loosened grip or false step would tip him onto the ground. This downhill balancing act was then followed by a risky river crossing. Carriers hoisted their loads high as they waded through the Little Big Horn, more than three feet deep in some places. By afternoon, while a few of the initially wounded men had returned to their companies, a balance of fifty-two patients had arrived at Gibbon's shady camp. The carriers judged their missions successful in terms of patient comfort. In the new field hospital, Doctors Porter, Paulding, and Williams measured the outcome by the extent of hemorrhage from the patients' wounds, and they quickly set to work to repair any damage done. Porter, long overdue for much needed sleep, that restorative state he had achieved only in very small increments during the previous several days, now confronted his most urgent task yet as he directed his orderlies to ready two men for surgical amputations.

Big Mike Madden was lying on an operating table of sorts—a piece of tentage spread on the ground—awaiting the amputation of his leg with the compound fracture. It would have been helpful to have the patient on a table or some sort of raised platform, allowing the surgeon to stand and maneuver his instruments freely and completely around an elevated leg. This was of particular importance for the quick, circular method of amputation.[10] But no such platform was available, and time was of the essence. Kneeling next to his patient lying flat on the ground, Porter's own position decidedly compromised his own freedom of movement, threatening physical awkwardness when he needed swift, efficient dexterity.

Few surgeons approached an amputation with anything but reluctance. Loss of any part of a limb was life altering for the patient, although it was usually better than the alternatives—inflammation, infection, pyemia, and most likely, death. Without question, part of Private Madden's leg was doomed for the grave, and the sooner Porter could remove the mangled portion of the limb and prepare the stump for proper drainage and eventual healing, the risk of life-threatening infection would lessen. While there was no option but to amputate, there were other decisions to be made. The surgeon had a choice of two methods of amputation: the circular method was the simplest, but the flap method provided greater comfort in a prosthesis. Generally, the circular procedure was also quicker, sometimes only three minutes from first cut to first bandage dressing. The remaining stump was raw and open, healing only as it granulated. But when a surgeon chose the flap method instead, he committed himself to more operating time and much more skill in finding uninjured tissue from which to make two healthy flaps for a decent-looking, more comfortable stump.

No one would have thought any less of Porter had he elected to perform a circular amputation of Madden's leg. Challenges to the operation already abounded, and the doctor could have opted to choose speed over finesse. But certain considerations disinclined Porter from using the circular method. His goals in this surgery—to save as much of the limb as possible, to use the healthiest skin and tissue to cover the two bones of the lower leg, and to work in favor of the patient's long-term comfort—all argued in favor of the flap method.[11] The choice of flaps—anterior/posterior or lateral—Porter knew would be determined largely by the nature and location of the private's wound.

Plied first with some medicinal whiskey, Madden then inhaled from the chloroform sprinkled onto a sponge held just above his nose and face. Interpreter Frank Gerard happened upon the scene in time to witness a second man faint. Unexpectedly, it was the men holding the sponge—not Madden—who first felt the effects of the chloroform, and out they went. Gerard mentioned to Porter his experience assisting frontier doctors, and the surgeon welcomed him by his side. Ultimately, it took the chloroform and another stiff drink to suppress and subdue a very anxious Madden. Porter quickly applied his Esmarch tourniquet around the patient's leg to cut off the blood flow and he set out instruments from his amputation kit.[12]

The initial incision lay a good inch below the place where Porter planned to saw the fibula and tibia bones. Crowded near him were three assistants: one to hold the limb steady, another to retract the skin and tissue as Porter incised further, and one to tie ligatures and sponge away blood and clots. Once he exposed the two bones, Porter used his surgical saw to etch a groove into them four inches below the knee. He wanted a clean cut with no bone splintering. He began to cut the larger bone first and then sawed both simultaneously. The severed part of the leg was shoved off to the side. Porter continued to work on the exposed bones in Madden's stump, clipping off sharp edges with a bone forceps and beveling the ends smooth. He tied off arteries. The original gunshot wound to Madden's leg had destroyed skin and tissue, back to front. Consequently, Porter created flaps from the lateral tissues of the leg, bringing the two side flaps together at the bottom of the stump with silk ligatures, leaving enough space for proper drainage of what he hoped would be only "laudable" pus. Assistants covered the stump with cotton and dressed it lightly. Most important, they knew to keep the limb elevated and protected from any physical pressure. The entire procedure was over in about ten minutes.[13]

Girard removed the chloroform sponge from above Madden's nose. To resuscitate his patient, Porter pulled forward the man's tongue to increase ventilation, then repeatedly lifted the patient's arms slowly over his head. Madden became conscious but remained quiet and looked ashen. There was no jollifying talk among the men about what had just happened. In the space of ten minutes, Porter had ended Madden's career in the cavalry and certainly excluded him from many other professions. None of this unsettled the surgeon, however—he simply hoped to save the man's life. The operation had been a success, but Porter knew that the healing process could be life threatening. A decade later Boston surgeon Arthur Tracy Cabot would be able to articulate better Porter's sense of misgiving: "Every surgical operation is an experiment in bacteriology."[14]

From Mike Madden's leg, Porter then moved on to his second amputation of the afternoon, this one on an entirely different scale but no less frightening to the patient. During the hilltop fight, Private John J. Phillips of Company H underwent surgery to remove several pieces of bone from his lower left jaw. It was now time for the surgeon to amputate the middle finger of his left hand between the first and second phalange; a single bullet had injured both the jaw and the finger as the soldier was aiming his carbine.[15] Again an orderly administered chloroform to the patient. Using smaller-scale instruments from his amputation kit, Porter completed the operation and hoped that he had spared the man the loss of his entire hand or more. Time would tell.

There was hardly a way to describe the physical and emotional exhaustion felt by all the men in Reno's battalion, wounded and healthy alike. But Private Daniel Newell gave it a try: "We were a pretty badly used up bunch of men," Newell told John P. Everett in 1930 during a rare interview. "Remember, we had ridden hard all day of the 24th and all the following night with only a short time to rest. Then riding and fighting all day of the 25th and all that night with no expectation of ever getting out alive, was all a human being could be expected to stand."[16] At the request of the surgeons, June 28 became a day of rest and recovery for the wounded. General Terry agreed to delay departure until late in the afternoon.

No one was left untouched by the gruesome aftermath of the battles. Captain Walter Clifford of the Seventh Infantry described the atmosphere: "The days are scorching hot and still, and the air is thick with the stench of festering bodies. We miss the laughing gaiety that usually attends a body of soldiery even on the battlefield. A brooding sorrow hangs like a pall over our every thought . . . and a dull, dogged feeling of revenge seems to be the prevailing senti- ment." The "festering bodies" of nearby dead horses again hosted swarms of green flies that were soon attracted to the meat cooking at the campfires. The insects set upon the men's food and squelched the appetite. They crawled over faces and eyes and buzzed into ears. Captain Clifford finally sought refuge at the river from the "repul- sive" flies and stench: "[O]ne is forced to lie with face close to the water to be rid of the deadly poison that is permeating the clothing and filling the lungs with every respiration. A little delay on this death-stricken ground and we will all remain forever."[17]

To prevent any further sag in morale around the camp, the offi- cers put all able-bodied men to work. Gibbon's soldiers set about making the hand and horse litters needed to transport the wounded fifteen miles down the Little Big Horn Valley to its mouth, where, on Terry's orders, the steamboat *Far West* was moored. The blanket and canvas materials of the first litters were discarded and replaced by more durable horsehides. It fell to Gibbon's men to kill the seriously wounded horses from Reno's battalion, just about the most unpleas- ant task for anyone in the cavalry since each man understood the affectionate bond established between horse and rider, many of whom had been together for years. "Eyes that followed in wonder- ing affection," one cavalryman feared, "would haunt him forever."[18] Once the horses were killed, soldiers stripped off their hides, dried the moisture out of them in the hot sunlight, and then cut them into long strips. They wound and wove the strips between two aspen poles into the form of a makeshift litter bed.

Work on the hand litters progressed well during the afternoon; the horse litters proved more difficult. In fact, they were designed to be mule litters because mules took smaller, steadier steps than horses.

Some of Gibbon's men labored with pairs of mules, training them to tolerate two tipi poles lashed to their sidesaddle packs, with a litter bed suspended between the poles. Mules may well have suited the litters due to their smaller body size and step; however, their famously obstinate disposition raised serious concerns for the safety of any man riding the litter between them. Depending on the direction of the patient's head, he could either be kicked by the rear legs of the mule in front or head-butted by the one in the rear.[19] The tedious training went on all afternoon.

Whatever the level of discomfort and frustration Gibbon's men felt in fulfilling their assigned tasks, it could hardly compare to the ordeal endured by the Seventh Cavalry survivors who were given a ghastly assignment: to bury Custer and the men of his annihilated battalion. Bodies of men they had known for years or even throughout a military career—comrades, friends, fathers of families—lay all across the hills and in the ravines, in clusters, in pairs, or sometimes painfully alone. The startling whiteness of their naked bodies was what first struck the eye, but this impression was quickly eclipsed by another: the degree of physical disfigurement. The three-day-old corpses were so swollen, bloated, blistered, and mutilated that identification was often impossible. In an effort to account for all the men in Custer's five companies, soldiers resorted to memories of personal details: tattoos, medals, unique boot heels, and even a pair of socks. Henry Porter anxiously searched for his colleague George Lord among the bodies. It was only when Doctor Williams, who had accompanied the cavalrymen in their somber duty, spied a pair of unbleached socks on a body that Lord was identified; Williams had been with him when the latter had purchased the socks from a sutler at the Powder River camp.[20] Porter had felt unstrung several times during the last forty-eight hours. But the gruesome sight now before him—Lord's bloated, rotting body—must have brought him up short. Porter comprehended that the sense of duty that had impelled George Lord to ride with Custer's battalion had spared his own life.

The gravediggers met resistance from the hard, dry soil. With only a few shovels available, most men resorted to using knife blades, tin cups, and their hands. In the end Custer and most of the thirteen officers received as complete a burial as was possible. Such was not the case, however, for most of the 193 enlisted men under the circumstances. Soldiers physically sickened by the grisly appearance of the bodies and the stench of decomposition often did little more than pile clumps of dirt, cuttings of sagebrush, and anything else at hand on top of their deceased comrades. The average enlisted man, recruited into the army with the promise of a decent meal in tough economic times, pay of thirteen dollars a month, and alluring stories of adventure, found it utterly incomprehensible that so many members of the once seemingly invincible Seventh Cavalry could meet such a horrifying end. Over time many survivors would resort to exaggerated spatial dimensions and amplified odds when retelling the story of the battle. The battlefield became mountainous or cut by deep ravines and canyons. The cavalry, it was said, had fought more than 10,000 well-armed warriors whose village spread out over five miles. In these exaggerations—reflecting their subjective observations as much as an intentional distortion of empirical reality—they sought to soothe their souls and save public face.[21]

The remaining seven companies of the Seventh Cavalry, now under the command of Major Reno, returned to the valley camp with a sole survivor of what became known as Custer's Last Stand. Comanche, a fourteen-year-old light bay horse ridden by Captain Keogh of Company I, was found by the river, shot five times but still alive. He nickered and came right away when his name was called. Private Dennis Lynch examined the bullet wounds—one above a forefoot hoof, two in the neck, one through the loins, and one in the chest. Lynch used a quill to blow into the chest wound and force discharge out of the obvious exit wound on the horse's side. Because the regimental veterinarian, C. A. Stein, had been left behind at the Powder River camp along with the musicians of the band, it fell to Lynch to dress the horse's wounds once back in camp. He did so with the same careful attention and tender touch that was afforded each of the wounded soldiers in the field hospital. Comanche's survival stirred feelings of steadfastness and pride in the men of the Seventh Cavalry. Without question, the horse would accompany them to the *Far West* and then ride the steamer to Fort Abraham Lincoln, destined to enjoy the same rest, recovery, and respect awaiting the wounded soldiers.[22]

During the day, surgeons in the field hospital waged their own battle of sorts. The decision to immobilize the wounded and prevent any recurrence of hemorrhage had, in turn, left them vulnerable to the harmful effects of the surrounding malignant air and swarms of filthy flies. Other than a dead body, nothing attracted a fly as much as a pus-filled wound. The surgeons' concerns reflected the still prevalent medical belief in 1876 that environment was largely the major source of disease. On the positive side, the belief had sponsored a greater emphasis on public health in the United States during the 1850s, especially in the cities. Remove "filth, crowding, poor ventilation, impure water, and bad drains," city officials believed, and "you can solve most health problems."[23] Initially it was a sensible and practical belief, but its acceptance as doctrine over the next several decades disinclined most American physicians from embracing the far more progressive "germ theory" of disease that was fast gaining acceptance among European medical communities.

The development of the germ theory of disease was truly an international effort. In the early 1860s, French physician and scientist Louis Pasteur had shown that it was not the air itself that was harmful but rather the "minute particles suspended in it which are the germs of various low forms of life" that settle everywhere. After reading Pasteur's work, English surgeon Joseph Lister realized that the airborne "germs" settled in wounds and caused putrefaction and pus creation. Kill the germs in the air and at the site of a wound, Lister reasoned, and you will prevent sepsis and infection. Conceiving the germ theory of disease led Lister to develop his antiseptic system of surgery using a carbolic spray. It was a complex, somewhat unwieldy system, but it significantly reduced the occurrence of postoperative infection in his patients. European physicians began experimenting with carbolic-acid spray after Lister published his findings in 1868. The next step was to prove and document a specific germ-disease relationship, which was accomplished by German physician Robert Koch when he identified the specific bacillus that caused anthrax. Originally a disease of animals, anthrax infected humans when skinning, butchering, or dissecting sick beasts. The cutaneous, or skin, form of anthrax presented with a painless blackened skin lesion that could progress to a fatal toxemia in the bloodstream. Koch identified the killer germ in 1876.[24]

The American medical community largely dismissed the notion of an inconceivably minute "germ" particle as "too liberal a use of the imagination."[25] Instead they remained wedded almost exclusively to an environmental explanation for disease and in so doing remained backward. Even worse, these men blinded themselves to other obvious agents of disease. By focusing only on the damp air carrying decaying plant effluvia from marshy and low-lying areas, U.S. physicians long overlooked the leading role played by mosquitoes in the transmission of malaria.

Henry Porter had good reason to express concern about the flies swarming around the hospital area: their feet added filth to everything they touched. But his preoccupation with atmospherics in the form of noxious vapors also indicated his acceptance of the parochial thinking of American medicine. Porter and his colleagues easily recognized disease, but they remained painfully ignorant of its source. Flies could not carry all the blame. The awful truth, as yet not comprehended by all, was that the dirty hands of physicians and their unwashed utensils served as much to transmit germs and disease as they did to tend and "cure" the patients. By late afternoon on June 28, the surgeons appealed to General Terry to move as soon as possible from the foul area for the sake of their pale-looking, septic patients.[26]

The columns of cavalry and infantry moved out in the cool of the evening at around 8:00 P.M. The drop in temperature added to the comfort of Porter's patients: colder air was known to restrict blood flow and help stop bleeding. Because of the mules' recalcitrance, there were a mere five mule litters in operation by departure time. All other patients either traveled on hand litters carried by two infantrymen or, where possible, rode horses. Private George Berry of the Seventh Infantry strained his 125-pound frame trying to carry a 185-pound man on a litter. The patient, shot in the back, begged not to be set down on the hard ground. Unfortunately for him, his sheer weight forced the two carriers to rest often and stumble along as they walked. The march was so tedious and slow—harrowing for all—that it was not long before General Terry assigned cavalrymen to assist the infantry and form four-man teams. One team carried the litter about fifty to sixty feet and then transferred the poles to the shoulders of the next team. In this revolving manner they managed to keep the litters off the ground and relieve the wounded of undue pain.[27]

As the evening darkened, the carriers often lost sure footing, further impeding progress. Gibbon was struck by the uncharacteristic dysfunction of the military column: "As we moved through the darkness, the silence of the night broken only by the tramp of men and horses and the groans of the suffering wounded, I could not help contrasting the scene presented with that gay spectacle we had witnessed only six days before, when Custer's splendid regiment moved out in solid column, with its guidons fluttering in the breeze as it disappeared from our sight over the bluffs at the mouth of the

Rosebud."[28] The colonel did not have long to reflect on the painful contrast. After marching a mere four miles, General Terry halted the column and ordered the men to camp for the night. They had gone barely a mile beyond the north end of the village site.

At least five men among the wounded had life-threatening wounds in addition to amputee Mike Madden. Their precarious conditions convinced Terry to reach the *Far West* as quickly as possible so they could start the long river journey to the hospital at Fort Abraham Lincoln and more-extensive medical care. On the morning of June 29, he asked for an alternative to the laborious hand litters. Gibbon eyed all the timber on the ground and suggested floating the wounded on rafts down the Little Big Horn.[29] Scouts in the command, who knew the river to be "narrow, shallow and torturous," reacted outright against the idea: no need for the wounded to suffer terror in addition to their pain.

This left only two alternatives: the Indian-style travois or the two-mule litter. The travois had long been used by roaming Indians to transport almost everything. Its design was simple: two tipi poles attached on either side of a saddle and extending behind an animal with the pole ends resting on the ground. The litter bed, woven of strips of hide between the two poles and then covered with blankets or buffalo robes, provided relative comfort for the passenger. A travois was drawn by one animal and required only one person to accompany it: an economical method when both men and horses were scarce. Already there were two travois in the column. An Arikara scout named Goose, his right hand severely injured, rode on one while the Crow scout White Swan, nursing wounds in his right wrist and thigh, occupied the other. While the Indians were entirely accustomed to this mode of travel, the army still had concerns about travois. Many officers had heard conflicting stories about soldiers who had ridden in such "primitive" conveyances. At best the jostling reminded one man of riding in a sleigh. Another soldier begged to differ: "Make this travois easier for me or kill me to get me out of my misery."[30]

Despite the simple construction of the travois and the economy of man and animal power, commanders still favored the two-mule litter, especially since 1st Lieutenant Gustavus C. Doane of Gibbon's Second Cavalry certified his ability to construct the devices and train the mules to carry them. His expertise derived from experience in two earlier evacuations of military wounded. Gibbon awarded Doane the job, and the soldier repaid him with what the colonel described as "zeal, skill and energy" for the duration of the project. The lieutenant's design for each litter required two sixteen-foot poles of green timber, which was more elastic, notched in specified places; two crosspieces to secure the poles three feet apart; and a lariat or rawhide thong to cord the bed space in a back-and-forth, zigzag manner. Sixteen-foot poles provided for a seven-foot-long bed space in the middle, leaving four and a half feet on either end: sufficient length to attach the front mule—always the smaller of the two—and to allow the animal in the rear position to see the path in front of his feet and not trip on obstacles and uneven ground.[31]

Lieutenant Doane instructed soldiers in the best practices for leading the mules into the litters. Although they had been carefully selected from the herd based on some evidence of docility, the mules still often behaved badly when first hitched up to the poles, settling down only after realizing that they could not break loose. Finally, Doane demonstrated how to make the animals maneuver with the litter between them. With a patient on board, it was a four-man job: one to lead each mule and another on each side of the litter bed to steady it and reattach any loosened ropes. Transporting the wounded on mule litters was not as backbreaking as moving them on hand litters, but it remained very labor intensive.

Late in the afternoon on June 29, soldiers carefully lifted the wounded onto the conveyances. The most severely impaired, including the two cases of amputation, a perforated knee joint, and four with penetrating wounds to the chest or abdomen, were placed on the mule litters. Ten other wounded men occupied travois pulled by single mules or horses. The remaining injured rode on gentle horses. Henry Porter supplied all his patients with pain-reducing opiates, but even so, the ride for some was uncomfortable. Private Peter Thompson, shot in the hand and forearm as a member of one of the water parties, "secured a horse that an earthquake could not excite." Nevertheless, it was a tough journey for him: "My head would spin round and I felt sick. I placed my head on the horse's neck and grasped his mane with my sound hand, hanging on for dear life."[32] Blood loss likely caused Thompson's lightheadedness and nausea. But at least he had the strength to hang onto the horse. Other patients were so weak, they could hardly sit up or stand and certainly could not grasp anything securely. These men hung suspended between two mules, their level of comfort dependent upon the success of the accompanying soldiers to cajole, bribe, and slap the animals into compliance.

The ambling procession had gone not too far down the valley before two couriers, dispatched twenty-four hours earlier, returned with welcome news about the *Far West*: the steamer was moored at the confluence of the Little Big Horn and the Big Horn Rivers, awaiting the soldiers and preparing for the wounded. Given the obvious difficulties of transporting such a large number of casualties, General Terry asked the couriers to map the shortest but easiest route to the boat. "As the crow flies" required that the columns cross the Little Big Horn twice as it snaked down the valley; hug the bluffs to a point at which they would scale them; cross a high, wide plateau; and finally descend from the plateau to the waiting steamboat.

To the surprise of most and the relief of Lieutenant Doane, the mule litters and travois worked well. When crossing the river, soldiers elevated the ends of the trailing poles that otherwise dragged along the ground. The mules tolerated the litter poles and burden suspended between them so well that Terry felt inclined to push through the evening and try to reach the *Far West* in the early morning. It also helped to have a young moon illuminating the terrain. The men felt relieved to be on the march again, but they were hardly relaxed. A column of soldiers strung out as they were along an unfamiliar path, ambulating at a cautious pace for the welfare of the wounded, was an easy target for an enemy attack. It was not at all difficult for members of the Seventh Cavalry to resurrect the feelings experienced during the timber and hilltop fights: echoes of that fear and helplessness still reverberated in most of them. Colonel Gibbon's cavalry and infantry had not only witnessed the grisly aftermath of this great battle but also were now responsible for the more than fifty men who bore the most painful physical effects of the fighting. Even though scouts had reassured Terry on June 27 that the enormous Indian gathering had moved southerly toward the snow-capped Big Horn Mountains, most men riding or walking under the general's command still mistrusted the surrounding landscape. Ascending the bluffs to a wide upland provided a sense of security that comes with elevation, but such relief proved short lived after heavy clouds moved in and obscured the moonlight; Gibbon described it as "dark as pitch."[33] The column suddenly lost the trail.

Darkness and the animals' skittishness quickly eroded military discipline. Cavalrymen collided with the foot soldiers, and Terry ordered bugles sounded to recover the fracturing column. Private Eugene Grant summed up the attitude of the inexperienced enlisted men: "It was dark, there were no roads, the mules were unruly, the wounded were groaning, and we were tired to death."[34] Fatigue also impaired their judgment and alarmed Grant: "If one man had fired a shot, one part of the command would have blazed into the other, thinking they were Indians." In the tumult of cavalry and infantry, animosities flared, with each military branch swearing about the ill placement of the other. Cavalry horses spooked and threatened to step on soldiers, many of whom wished they had their bayonets handy to remind the cavalrymen to keep their distance.

Amid the ill-tempered soldiers, the wounded were entirely help-less and further exhausted from fear and pain. Small collisions agitated the mules and forced the litters to move at awkward angles. Finally, a misstep by one mule into a prairie-dog hole caused one litter to tip so precipitously that its passenger fell off. It took several strong soldiers to lift Private Madden off the cactus-strewn ground and place him back on his litter. Madden had survived the fighting of the twenty-fifth and had endured unimaginable pain both before and since the amputation of his leg two days later. By June 29 a spill onto the ground among some cacti could hardly agitate him. Opium helped mitigate his discomfort, and for that Doctor Porter was no doubt grateful. But there was little the surgeon could do in the dark and confusion to check on the state of the private's leg. Porter knew that a spill such as Madden had just taken could easily have broken open the flaps of skin covering his amputated limb, risking bleed-ing and infection, for the stump had barely begun to heal in the two days since surgery. The surgeon's goals were to strengthen his patient with fortifying beef broth and, at all costs, keep the stump clean and free of infection with proper drainage and dressings. He could accomplish none of this until the command reached the *Far West*. For now, Porter could only stand by while scouts groped for the trail and hope that order would be restored in the column.

Instead, the darkness only intensified, and it began to rain. The couriers could not make out the path they had followed just hours earlier. Resistant to any thought of bivouacking for the night on that exposed plateau with no proper shelters for all the wounded, Gen-eral Terry appealed to the Indian scouts for help. Half Yellow Face, guiding the travois carrying the wounded White Swan, his fellow Crow, moved to the front of the column and hunted for the trail in the darkness and rain. In time the men glimpsed a light below them in the distance but could not determine what kind of terrain lay in between it and them. The entire command halted while Gibbon and a staff officer dismounted and picked their way down the hillside. The noise of their descent alerted an unknown party below; a shouted exchange of military identities confirmed that Gibbon had found the correct path. Climbing from below was Captain Stephen Baker and some men of the Sixth Infantry, who had been detailed to protect the steamboat. As they continued their ascent, Gibbon picked his way down the steep hillside past them to the boat below. It would be a treacherous descent for the wounded-bearing mules, unable to see the ground before them. The colonel was convinced that many of the wounded could not endure another such terrifying test. The obvious solution would be to illuminate the path. With torches from the boat, a group of men started small fires along the edge of the trail, working their way up the hillside. Once beaded with light from the fires, the descending path became less of a challenge for the column. It was now early morning on June 30, and every member of Terry's command was desperate to reach the boat below, deliver the wounded on board, collapse into sleep, and in the words of Captain Clifford, "shut out for a time the sickening picture that has been ever present since the 27th."[35]

The *Far West,* moored at the eastern bank of the Big Horn River just above its confluence with the Little Big Horn, shone in the light of many pine torches set up along the riverside. She was a welcoming haven and a reminder to all of a more accommodating and civilized life. The steamboat captain, Grant Marsh, had been preparing for the wounded for two days, long enough for his crew to cut fresh grass and pile it approximately a foot and a half deep on the main deck. Once covered with canvas tarpaulins, the area became an enormous, sweet-smelling mattress. The result of this effort satisfied Porter that his patients finally would be comfortable. By dawn forty of them plus the two wounded Indian scouts were settled aboard the boat. The balance of the original fifty wounded men had recovered well enough to rejoin their companies and encamp on the riverbank.

As the doctor checked on his patients in the floating field hospital, he gave each the immense pleasure of a stiff drink of whiskey.

True to his word, Colonel Gibbon had made sure that the army never left the wounded behind. Satisfied with the evacuation, he joined General Terry and his staff aboard the *Far West,* where all promptly retired to sleeping quarters in cabins on the boiler deck. As they reached the riverbank, officers and enlisted men of the column disregarded nearly all procedures for setting up camp. Their exhaustion was overwhelming. As soon as a man found a clear opening, he was on the ground and asleep. Even picketed horses were almost too tired to graze on the lush grass covering the bottomland.

Captain Marsh aimed to secure the comfort of all on board his boat. In the dawning light he witnessed the wounded men bed down in the makeshift hospital while the senior officers retreated into rooms on the second deck. Then he paid attention to one very unique patient. As Marsh's biographer, Joseph P. Hanson, later wrote about Comanche: "with such tender interest and affection was he already regarded by every man on board that they would almost rather have been left behind themselves than to have had him deserted."[36] Soldiers led Comanche to the stern of the boat, where Marsh quickly improvised a stall between the rudders. As the wounded horse lay down on the thickly piled grass, the captain felt satisfied with his efforts to receive and accommodate every last survivor of the Battle of the Little Big Horn.

8

The *Far West*

ALFRED TERRY HAD NOT ALWAYS BEEN A MILITARY MAN. Before the Civil War and the start of his military career, he had practiced law successfully in Connecticut. The attorney in him was still manifest in his thoughtful demeanor, his meticulous preparations and plans, and (perhaps above all) his careful choice of words. On the morning of June 30, Terry requested Captain Marsh's attendance in his private cabin onboard the *Far West*. The steamboat captain set aside his launching preparations and obliged the general. Terry closed the door to his small upper-deck room and made his request of Marsh: "Captain, you are about to start on a trip with 52 wounded men on your boat. This is a bad river to navigate and accidents are liable to happen. I wish to ask of you that you use all of the skill you possess, all of the caution you can command, to make the journey safely." He concluded with a sober verdict: "Captain, you have on board the most precious cargo a boat ever carried. Every soldier here who is suffering with wounds is the victim of a terrible blunder; a sad and terrible blunder."[1]

It had been four days since Terry and Colonel Gibbon had discovered the fate of the Seventh Cavalry. In that time the general had been obliged to sort out the events of the campaign. All around him, such terms as "massacre," "disobedience," and "abandonment" flavored conversations. Terry, however, condensed the Battle of the Little Big Horn into a decidedly neutral term: "blunder." In his meeting with Captain Marsh, he steered clear of assigning blame for the outcome of the battle, focusing instead on the urgent task at hand: the need to end the hemorrhaging of the regiment by delivering its wounded soldiers to safety and care at the hospital at Fort Abraham Lincoln. Terry's appeal to Marsh for a safe journey derived from his genuine compassion for the suffering men. Beyond that, his few words approached the sound of a prayer in which he quietly and privately asked for relief from the near incomprehensibility of such an unfortunate, seemingly pointless loss of life. Despite Terry's meticulous planning for the campaign, a "terrible blunder" had indeed occurred, resulting in the deaths of 270 men—nearly one-half of the regiment and one percent of the entire U.S. Army.[2] The survival of those clinging to life on the *Far West* was critical for both obvious and more subtle reasons, but most particularly it would help assuage Terry's own feelings of regret and sadness.

The power of Terry's words—"most precious cargo" and "victims of a terrible blunder"—found their true emotional mark only when Marsh returned to his pilothouse. Shaken by the solemnity of the general's request, Marsh confessed to a fellow boatman an uncharacteristic crisis of confidence. To transport the wounded men safely to Fort Abraham Lincoln, over 700 miles away, would be an exploit; to do so with the speed and urgency demanded by their medical conditions would require heroic effort.

The *Far West* would also return the personal effects of the dead officers to wives and families. Marsh and his boat would thereby serve as a conduit between the dead and the living, a thought that further unnerved him. In stark contrast he recalled the afternoon of May 27—only thirty-four days earlier—when he moored his vessel at Fort Abraham Lincoln to load supplies for the coming campaign. The Seventh Cavalry had already departed for Montana, leaving behind wives in need of simple distractions. The ladies ambled aboard the steamboat as an excursion. Always the gentleman, Marsh ordered a luncheon prepared for them and served in the boat's formal dining room. Their delight at his thoughtfulness pleased him. Now on June 30 this happy memory was obscured by his painful awareness of the "cargo" he would be carrying back to them. The captain knew that he needed a steely composure to navigate the hundreds of miles of the Yellowstone and Missouri ahead while keeping at bay thoughts of the dead and sympathy for the suffering that crowded his head and strained his nerves.

Marsh now brought all his thirty years of experience working aboard steamboats to the challenge confronting him. Without a doubt, the *Far West* was well suited for the important journey ahead. Described as "one of the river greyhounds" by Joseph Mills Hanson, Captain Marsh's biographer, the *Far West* enjoyed a reputation as one of the fastest boats on the western rivers. She was 190 feet long and a slim 33 feet wide, carrying three wood-burning boilers, two engines, and a waterwheel in the stern. As such, she was built for speed and the demanding conditions of the northern rivers. Filled to her capacity of 400 tons, the vessel drew four feet, six inches of water; unloaded, she drew a mere twenty inches. Her shallow draught facilitated speed; it was said with pride that the *Far West* could "navigate on a heavy dew." In 1876, Marsh had chosen this craft over another regaled boat—the *Josephine*—because it was such a light, speedy, strong workhorse, perfect for transporting supplies, transferring soldiers back and forth across the treacherous Yellowstone, and maintaining critical communication between commands spread out from the Powder River to the Little Big Horn.[3]

Just after noon on June 30 and under a light rain, the *Far West* departed, heading for the Yellowstone, fifty-three miles away down the Big Horn. Marsh and his crew were now able to get a second look at the obstacles that had impeded their upriver journey just days before. On that trip Marsh masterfully maneuvered the steamboat around numerous small islands and shifting sandbars. The water had been so shallow in places that Marsh doubted if he could "go over the same route in a skiff." Occasionally the rapids they encountered proved too much for the power of the boat's stern wheel, bringing the vessel almost to a standstill. The crew resorted to a warping method for additional power, dragging a thick warping cable ashore and wrapping it around a large tree. Deckhands attached the other end of the cable to one of the boat's capstans up near the bow. As soldiers revolved this spool-shaped cylinder, it hauled in the warping cable and dragged the boat forward. Where the river was not too wide, they attached cables to trees on both banks and used both capstans to pull the boat along. Here too the *Far West* proved best suited for the route since she was the first steamboat built with more than one capstan.[4]

Now traveling downriver, Marsh and his crew were happy to be relieved of the grueling labor that had been required to drag the boat upstream. But the rapid downstream current forced the captain and his copilot to make split-second decisions to steer away from fast-approaching islands, sandbars, riverbanks, and snags. At all costs Marsh tried to avoid contact with anything stationary so as not to jostle and jolt his passengers. Even so, according to the testimony of 2nd Lieutenant Charles Roe of Gibbon's cavalry, still bivouacked along the banks of the Big Horn River and who watched the *Far West* maneuver downriver, "we could see it actually waltz down the river, striking the banks repeatedly, first the stern and then the bow."[5] For the wounded men onboard, these collisions may have raised anxiety levels and caused actual physical pain.

The *Far West* reached the Yellowstone River late in the day and moored along the bank adjacent to Gibbon's supply wagons. For two days the steamboat lingered at the mouth of the Big Horn, serving as headquarters for General Terry and his staff and as hospital for Doctor Porter and his sickly and distraught patients. While Doctor Williams had accompanied Terry downriver, Doctor Paulding had remained with Gibbon and Reno, who marched overland with their columns of infantry and cavalry from the Little Big Horn. Upon their arrival, the *Far West* would ferry them across the Yellowstone to the north bank, where they would encamp and await supplies and reinforcements before continuing the summer campaign against the Sioux.

Porter understood the necessity for this two-day layover but nevertheless regretted the delay in reaching Fort Abraham Lincoln. It had been one week since the battle, seven days of pain and suffering for the wounded. Of the forty-two men still under his care, the surgeon worried particularly about five patients, fully aware that infection was a continuing threat. On July 2 Corporal George H. King of Company A died of the gunshot wound in his left shoulder, sustained during Reno's hilltop fight. His comrades buried the twenty-eight-year-old soldier on the north bank of the Yellowstone opposite the mouth of the Big Horn. Corporal King was the first to die since the evacuation began.

Late on July 2, able soldiers carefully transferred all of the wounded men from the boat to a makeshift camp built under the cottonwood shade along the riverbank. Gibbon's Montana column and the Seventh Cavalry survivors had arrived, and the *Far West* ferried the men and horses across the wide Yellowstone to its north side. By 10:00 P.M. the steamer had transported the last of the soldiers. The boat crew cleaned the deck of mud and manure and once again transformed their vessel into a floating hospital, piling fresh-cut grass and tarpaulins beneath the upper deck and returning the medicine chests on deck for Porter and his orderlies. Cords of wood piled four feet high rimmed the outer edges of the main deck. On average a steamboat burned twenty-five cords of wood for every twenty-four hours of steaming. Captain Marsh intended to steam around the clock to get the patients to Bismarck and Fort Abraham Lincoln. The stacks of wood and piled sacks of grain also offered protection for the wounded. In its many capacities the *Far West* served the U.S. Army very well in 1876, and for her services that summer the owners received $360 per day.[6]

Marsh set off at about noon on July 3, intending to reach Bismarck in record time. Onboard, in addition to the boatmen, were Captain Edward W. Smith, aide-de-camp to General Terry; Doctor Porter; several attendants supporting Porter; forty-two patients; seventeen soldiers of the Seventh Cavalry who had lost their horses in battle and now provided protection for the boat; and the wounded horse Comanche. The month of July marked about the middle of the short navigation season that typically ran from late May to mid-August. At that time of year, Marsh knew he had the advantages of long daylight hours and snowmelt-fed high waters in the rivers. Even so, he warned all onboard that the rushing current could at any moment jam the keel of the boat into a submerged sandbar and send all on the decks reeling over. The daunting task of pairing speed with safety would keep Marsh and his copilot alternating in four-hour shifts in the wheelhouse, "scanning the water in front for the faintest riffle of hidden snag or shoaling bar."[7]

Henry Porter had tended to his patients in many difficult conditions over the previous eight days. Heat, thirst, unsteady horses, flies, vapors, and the behavior of fractious mules had constituted some of the threats to these men. He hesitated to add their journey on the *Far West* to the list, relieved as he was to be underway at last. But everyone onboard could have rightfully regarded the journey ahead as nothing short of perilous, their safety endangered by countless unseen obstacles in the water, sharpshooting Indians hidden anywhere along the banks, and the ever-possible explosion of a steam boiler.

Only a few miles downriver, the *Far West* confronted an unusual spectacle. The Yellowstone River in front of the boat had turned black, filled with an immense herd of buffalo thrusting its way through the water toward the opposite bank. So near did the boat approach that crewmembers on deck could touch the animals with the ten-foot measuring pole normally used to sound the depths of rivers. Initially, Captain Marsh slowed the steamer near the bank, planning to wait out the herd's crossing. He underestimated its size, however, and with critical time passing, he eventually nosed the boat carefully through the massive herd. From then on it was full steam ahead to the boat's first stop, the army's supply camp at the mouth of the Powder River.[8]

Care for the wounded generally improved after the men were bedded down on the *Far West*. Although Porter was the sole medical officer onboard, he employed the service of several soldier-orderlies for the routine dressing of wounds and daily care of the patients. Water was readily available for cleansing, drinking, and cooking the beef broth that nourished the weakened men. Medicinal supplies were ample. Compared to the various conditions he had worked under since June 25, this floating hospital served magnificently. Its relative comfort certainly contributed to that mysterious process of healing, the progress of which appeared in external signs: light-colored or minimal pus in a wound, lessening skin redness around the damaged area, absence of pain or fever, overall good pallor, and an increasing appetite for food. Porter was heartened by what he observed in his patients, reassured that his diligence in wound care was serving the unfortunate men well. Each day allowed the skin around their wounds to granulate and close a little more, creating a natural barrier to infection.

For some, however, the rate of infection still surpassed the healing process, holding in check granulation and skin closure. The wounds of such men remained red, raw, and painful, the pus ugly and foul smelling. The more lethargic the patient, the more Porter suspected that infection was stealing throughout the man's body and well beyond his medical reach. All he could do was fortify the man with beef broth, "stimulate" his system with medicinal whiskey, and then simply hope that a sound constitution prevailed. For Porter, the waiting was always more difficult than the demanding work. The mystery of infection seemed to ridicule his hard-earned medical knowledge and toy with his dedicated efforts.

Private William George of Company H begged the doctor for

opiate to stop the pain from the wound in his left side. Over the eight days since George had been shot in the hilltop fight, the infection-laden projectile caused increasing abdominal pain and fever, exhausting the patient and taxing the efforts of his physician. The bullet and all the debris it had carried were still lodged inside the man's body. Porter could have anticipated the onset of peritonitis in George's case since the wound sat so close to the stomach and digestive organs. He administered the opium to his patient more as a last rite than as a palliative agent. William George died at 4:00 A.M. on July 3. Private Daniel Newell was bedded down next to George on the deck and observed firsthand his death. What he saw hardly corresponded to the description of peritonitis described years later in 1884 in *The Soldier's Handbook*: "the person lives a day or two, with perfect clearness of intellect and often not suffering greatly." Private George had exhibited enough "clearness of intellect" for eight days to know that he was suffering—greatly.[9]

Deckhands brought George's body ashore at the Powder River depot, the supply camp established by General Terry on June 6. When the *Far West* moored along the bank on July 4, its arrival interrupted a series of volleys being fired by the soldiers stationed there as they observed the national holiday in the nation's centennial year. Until then these men had heard only fragmented accounts of the Battle of the Little Big Horn from the Indian scouts who had been with the Seventh Cavalry but had chosen not to join the fight. The arrival of the *Far West* suddenly made it possible to learn the rest of the story. For the stunned soldiers in the camp, a three-company battalion of the Sixth Infantry, and for those working on the steamboat, there were no pleasantries to exchange during the two-hour layover.[10]

Private George was buried with honors. The boatmen then retrieved and loaded the personal possessions stowed at the depot belonging to the Seventh Cavalry officers killed in battle. One patient went ashore to the depot hospital, and in exchange the soldier who had accidentally shot himself in the foot on June 6 and a few other ailing men came on board. The floating hospital also gained the services of Doctor Isaiah Ashton, one of two surgeons then on duty there. His availability now to help care for the wounded for the duration of the trip to Fort Abraham Lincoln was a godsend to Doctor Porter. It may have been the only bright moment in the short layover before the *Far West* steamed off again. In its wake the Powder River depot remained in mourning, and its Independence Day celebrations were carried out in a pall.

"We ran out of the mouth of the Yellowstone and entered the Missouri," wrote Bob Burleigh, clerk of the *Far West,* in his diary on July 4. Near the confluence of the two rivers, the steamer stopped briefly at Fort Buford. There two ailing soldiers who had not seen any combat disembarked, one with consumption, the other with severe constipation. Again the boat headed downstream, still 310 miles from Bismarck but moving under full boiler pressure at an average rate of 13 miles per hour. Goose, the Ree scout with the injured hand, went ashore at Fort Berthold and was welcomed by his Arikara people. Downstream the *Far West* also docked at Fort Stevenson, the last formal stop before Bismarck. It was the afternoon of July 5.[11]

Among the directives General Terry had given Captain Marsh was to drape the boat's derrick and jack staff in black and hoist the flag at half-mast before reaching Bismarck.[12] Marsh chose Fort Stevenson as the logical place to carry out these orders. At about the same time, another of Doctor Porter's patients died, the third since the wounded men came aboard the steamer. Private James Bennett of Company C had been shot in the spine and paralyzed completely below the injury. Although he suffered minimal physical pain, he had agonized over his incapacitation, and for even his most basic functions, he depended entirely on the care of the orderlies. It was perhaps fortunate that he felt no sensation in the lower part of his body because the J-shaped, inflexible, silver catheter they inserted many times to allow him to urinate might otherwise have caused him to swear like the devil. Bennett's death did not really surprise Porter, nor could he feel especially saddened, knowing the kind of life the young man faced had he survived; by comparison, the future for Private Madden with his amputated leg looked positively cheery. Bennett's wrapped body remained aboard, awaiting a formal burial at Fort Abraham Lincoln.

At about 11:00 P.M. on July 5, the *Far West* approached Bismarck under bright moonlight. The early July days had been very warm, forcing many residents to shun the stuffy bedrooms in their homes and sleep outdoors instead.[13] The sound of the steamboat's paddle-wheel churning through the water drew their attention; the black drapes and half-mast flag left them thunderstruck. Once again the *Far West* succeeded in jolting a community with its dreadful tidings.

Those aboard the steamboat perceived their arrival differently. They had just completed a record-setting voyage, traveling nearly 710 miles in fifty-four hours with no mishaps. The concentration, skill, and stamina of the captain and his copilot were matched only by the physical endurance of the shirtless crewmembers, who had continually fed wood into the furnaces and kept a watchful eye on the steam gauges that had often recorded dangerously high pressure in the boilers. Marsh had carried out Terry's directive to deliver a "precious cargo" safely. He took pride in thinking that his efforts equaled those of the young surgeon working around the clock on the deck with, as Marsh later told reporters, "the coolness of the oldest veterans, shunning no danger and leaving nothing undone which might alleviate the sufferings of the wounded." For his part, Henry Porter surely felt comparable praise and gratitude for the steamboat captain, whose record speed on the Yellowstone and Missouri helped ensure against the loss of additional wounded. By morning the post surgeons at Fort Abraham Lincoln's hospital, Major and Surgeon Johnson V. D. Middleton and his assistant, Acting Assistant Surgeon Robert G. Redd, would inherit their care and afford them the true rest and detailed medical attention that conditions and circumstances had made impossible every day since June 25.[14]

Among the many people awakened by the clamor in the streets of Bismarck that night were Colonel Clement A. Lounsberry, editor of the *Bismarck Times,* and J. M. Carnahan, the local telegraph operator. Both were needed to transmit official military reports to headquarters in Saint Paul and Chicago. Captain Smith, Terry's aide-de-camp, along with Captain Marsh, and Doctor Porter hurried together with the editor and telegraph operator to open the newspaper office and commence a marathon transmission of information. First in line was Terry's dispatch to division headquarters at Chicago. Then Carnahan keyed the story and supplemental interviews that Lounsberry conducted with Smith, Porter, Marsh, and others to the *New York Herald* and other newspapers.[15]

As fast as Lounsberry prepared news copy, Carnahan fingered the telegraph key. Theirs was the story of a shocking defeat suffered by the U.S. Army, provocatively headlined "Massacred." The telegraph lines hummed from Bismarck to Fargo, where the operator there immediately detected the "fist" of J. M. Carnahan, whose tapping mannerisms were as distinctive as fingerprints. From Fargo the story sped to Saint Paul and then to New York City. Lounsberry wrote copy at a frantic pace, intent upon getting a scoop. When there was a lull in Carnahan's transmission, because his telegraphic speed had outstripped Lounsberry's wordsmithing, the editor threw a copy of the *New Testament* onto the operator's table and ordered him to use its text as a placeholder: "Fire it in when you run out of copy. Hold the wires. Tell 'em it's coming and to hold the key."[16]

In the mad clicking of the telegraph, Henry Porter heard much more than a mere mechanical noise: "what [Carnahan] sent vibrating around the world is history," he thought. Toward dawn and long after Smith, Marsh, and Porter had returned to the *Far West,* Carnahan remained at the key, subsisting on coffee and sandwiches and periodically blotting his forehead with a wet towel. Over the course of twenty-one hours, he transmitted more than 15,000 words, at a cost to the *New York Herald* of $3,000; for his efforts Carnahan earned $50. The *Herald* would likely sell five times its normal circulation thanks to the story of this shocking battle.[17]

Only a few hours after her arrival in Bismarck, the *Far West* steamed up once again for the short trip to Fort Abraham Lincoln. Along the way Doctors Porter and Ashton and their orderlies prepared the wounded soldiers for the final transfer to the post hospital. Many anticipated the comforts of cleanliness, warmth, and garrison food other than hardtack, bacon, and coffee. Some dreaded inevitable surgery and more pain ahead. A few were haunted by the thought that the post hospital might be their final resting place. It had been forty-four days since they had departed the fort, supremely confident that there was no one in the American West who could defeat the Seventh Cavalry.[18]

Arriving at Fort Abraham Lincoln in the early morning, Porter and Ashton escorted their remaining thirty-eight patients to the post hospital. The wooden rectangular building sat east of the cavalry parade ground. The hospital was designed for maximum light and ventilation since fresh air was considered the most effective countermeasure to unhealthy miasmas. Tall windows looked out upon a wrap-around roofed veranda. Small windows running along the cupola on the roofline provided additional natural light for the two wards inside. Interior whitewashed walls suggested cleanliness. In all, it was a pleasant structure to behold, although it was not held to any standard of longevity. In general the army considered the lifespan of a post hospital temporary at best, expecting to rebuild it when it had become "thoroughly saturated with hospital poison." What Hippocrates had called "erysipelas," Civil War surgeons had named "hospital gangrene." Both were describing a process by which, it was believed, miasmas or poisonous substances spread atmospherically from patient to patient and wound to wound, causing a rapid, ugly, fetid dissolution of tissues surrounding the injury. The process was often lethal. It followed that these same airborne toxins also permeated the hospital building itself, inevitably saturating the wood well beyond the cleansing power of fresh air or whitewash.[19]

Despite the building's pleasant appearance and promise of respite and possible cure, the wounded soldiers entering the post hospital likely experienced some apprehension, for they were aware that such buildings often carried the reputation for harboring harmful miasmas. Meanwhile, the body of James Bennett was delivered to the Dead House, just behind the hospital, to await interment.[20]

Doctor Middleton, the senior physician in the garrison, received the wounded men and conferred with Porter and Ashton about the nature and status of the various wounds. The discussion, conducted in medical and technical language, required that Porter suddenly adopt a degree of distance from his patients, men he had nursed intensively for ten days, some since they first arrived on the hilltop to fall off their horses in exhaustion and pain. It was a strange transition. He could appreciate that the men would now receive proper care. Middleton could examine their wounds and probe for bullets and foreign matter in places that Porter had felt were too risky to explore in the rough, dirty environment of the field. Middleton could extract foreign bodies and suture incisions. Ether and chloroform would give the surgeon time to do his work carefully and relieve his patients of any awareness of their surgeries. Middleton had medical supplies and working conditions that Porter had lacked in the field. Yet the contract surgeon also understood that there was very little that Middleton could administer to these men for the trauma they had suffered and the sadness they carried over friends lost and lives dramatically altered.

Hospital orderlies quickly went to work peeling and cutting from the wounded soldiers shreds of trail-worn clothing and bandages.

After a proper cleansing, each patient was provided with new underwear; even those in considerable pain relished the hygienic transformation. Satisfied with their conditions, Porter took leave of the men and the hospital, utterly exhausted. After resting, he would find Captain Marsh and learn of his new orders.

Not all of the wounded onboard the *Far West* were delivered to Fort Lincoln. The cavalry horse Comanche was let off the steamer at Bismarck and stabled in John W. Mellet's local livery.[21] In the city his status as the "lone survivor" of a battle that few could yet comprehend continued to afford the horse extraordinary care and attention, not to mention nutritious oats for the duration of his stay. It was considered a true honor to restore the horse to health and ready him to reunite with the Seventh Cavalry when the regiment returned at the close of the summer campaign.

During the short trip from Bismarck to Fort Abraham Lincoln, most onboard the *Far West* had concentrated on delivering the wounded men to the hospital. This practical focus helped to offset their awareness of the profound grief their arrival would occasion. Bob Burleigh, clerk of the steamer, recorded this anxiety in his diary: "I expect the scene will be a most heart-rendering one, as there are 21 women at the fort who will be husbandless tomorrow morning, for the first time to their knowledge, though they have been since the 25th of last month."[22] Libbie Custer, wife of George Armstrong Custer, became the post's, and soon America's, most famous widow. Maggie Calhoun suffered the loss of five family members: her husband, 1st Lieutenant James Calhoun; her three brothers, George, Tom and Boston Custer; and her nephew, Harry Armstrong Reed. The young men—Boston Custer and Harry Reed—had been visitors for the summer, glad to take in the fresh western air and anxious to see their famous kin—"General" George and Captain Tom—in action. Boston and Harry were invited to join the campaign and had been assigned to the pack train and the cattle herd, respectively. Both had disregarded their assignments on June 25 and had ridden off instead with Custer's battalion, anticipating a colorful adventure. Another of the sad widows at the fort was Annie Yates, wife of Captain George Yates, alone now with their three small children, ages four years, two years, and eight months.

On July 8, two days after receiving the dreadful news, Libbie Custer dispatched Doctor Middleton to the *Far West* with an invitation for Grant Marsh, asking that the captain visit her and the other grieving widows.[23] It was still difficult for Marsh to accept the deaths of so many friends among the officers and soldiers in the Seventh Cavalry, and it was impossible for him to fathom the grief and sudden emptiness felt by the widows. Libbie's invitation so clashed with his fond memory of their shared luncheon on May 27 that Captain Marsh was forced to send his regrets. There were limits to his bravery.

Henry Porter spent his few brief days in Bismarck gathering supplies, both personal and medical. He also saw to it that his family was made aware of his own survival. During the layover at the Powder River depot on July 4, he had written his parents a harrowing account of his role in the battle. It joined other letters in the mail pouch that Captain Smith delivered to the Bismarck post office on July 5. Anticipating that his parents might read the account of the Little Big Horn in a newspaper before they received his letter, Porter wisely sent a telegram to them in New York Mills. On July 7 Doctor Henry Norton Porter and his wife, Helen, received the most joyous news about their son: "Henry arrived safe in charge of wounded men after a terrible battle."[24]

What was not said in the telegram, however, was that young Porter, still on duty as a contract surgeon with the Seventh Cavalry in the summer campaign against the Sioux, had embarked on the *Far West* on July 9 for a return voyage up the Missouri and

Yellowstone Rivers to the mouth of the Big Horn, where General Terry remained in camp. The vessel steamed up the rivers carrying tons of supplies for the army columns in the field. The place on deck where Porter had previously tended forty-two wounded and dying soldiers was now occupied by miscellaneous equipment, including sixty cavalry horses.

Henry Renaldo Porter, possibly twenty years old. Courtesy
State Historical Society of North Dakota, 0264–012.

Acting Assistant Surgeon Henry Renaldo Porter.
Courtesy State Historical Society of North Dakota, 0264–008.

Porter's army contract with the "Expedition against hostile Sioux."
Courtesy National Archives.

Porter's surgical pocket case.
Courtesy State Historical Society of North Dakota, 2052.

Porter's field kit.
Courtesy State Historical Society of North Dakota, 15202.

Acting Assistant Surgeon
James Madison DeWolf.
Courtesy National Park Service,
Little Bighorn Battlefield National
Monument.

Assistant Surgeon and 1st
Lieutenant George Edwin Lord.
Courtesy National Park Service,
Little Bighorn Battlefield
National Monument.

Assistant Surgeon and 1st Lieutenant Holmes Offley Paulding. Courtesy National Library of Medicine.

Steamer *Far West* at Cow Island, Missouri River, Montana. Courtesy Institute for Regional Studies, North Dakota State University, Fargo.

Captain Grant Marsh.
Courtesy Montana Historical
Society Research Center–
Photograph Archives, Helena.

Stretcher with wounded man from the Battle of Slim Buttes, 1876.
Courtesy Library of Congress.

Brigadier General Alfred H. Terry, commander of the Department of Dakota. Courtesy National Archives.

Brigadier General George Crook, commander of the Department of the Platte. Courtesy National Archives.

Major Marcus A. Reno,
Seventh Cavalry.
Courtesy Montana Historical
Society Research Center–
Photograph Archives, Helena.

Captain Frederick W. Benteen,
Seventh Cavalry.
Courtesy Montana Historical
Society Research Center–
Photograph Archives, Helena.

Lieutenant Colonel George A. Custer, Seventh Cavalry. Courtesy National Archives.

Colonel John Gibbon, Seventh Infantry. Courtesy National Archives.

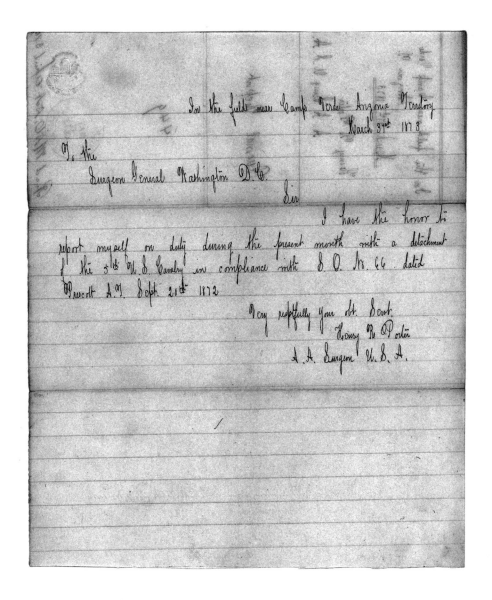

In the field near Camp Verde Arizona Territory
March 31st 1873

To the
Surgeon General Washington D.C.

Sir

I have the honor to report myself on duty during the present month with a detachment of the 5th U.S. Cavalry in compliance with S.O. No. 66 dated Prescott A.T. Sept. 20th 1872

Very respectfully your obt. Servt.
Henry R. Porter
A.A. Surgeon U.S.A.

Porter's monthly report to the surgeon general, March 31, 1873.
Courtesy National Archives.

Camp on Big Horn River
June 30th 1876

To the
Surgeon General
U. S. Army
Washington. D. C.
Sir

I have the honor to report that I am and have been on duty with the Expedition against hostile Sioux Indians, in compliance with Contract made with Commanding General Department of Dakota, at Fort A. Lincoln. D. T. May 15th 1876, during the month of June 1876.

Very Respectfully, Sir
Your obedient Servant
H. R. Porter
A. A. Surgeon. U.S.A.

Porter's monthly report to the surgeon general, June 30, 1876.
Courtesy National Archives.

Part III

Aftermath

9

More Than Bullets Can Harm

HENRY PORTER ADDRESSED THE ENVELOPE "Mrs. Dr. DeWolf" and began his letter, "Dear Madame." He took it upon himself to compose a condolence message to Fanny DeWolf, widow of fellow contract surgeon and friend James DeWolf.

It was customary in the army for officers and soldiers to narrate their comrades' deaths in letters sent to wives, parents, or next of kin. The letters, beyond verifying the sad news, often served to reassure the living about the benign circumstances of their loved one's death. Accordingly, Porter chronicled the retreat from the timber, the Little Big Horn crossing, the ascent of the bluffs, and how DeWolf turned up a ravine just to the left of the one Porter and most others chose to climb. It was his friend's absence from the hilltop a short while later that aroused Porter's concern; the discovery of the surgeon's body soon after caused him heartache. But, he emphasized for the widow in accordance with custom, her husband's death had been instantaneous—he had not suffered. Indians had not mutilated his body, had not scalped him, and had not taken his clothes. The upstanding man Fanny DeWolf had known in life had died undefiled. Porter wanted the widow to remember her husband as she knew him and to imagine him moving on to a peaceful afterlife, physically intact and even properly dressed. Such details of propriety, he knew, often lessened the ache of loss by stirring other, more consoling emotions.

Thanks to Porter's missive, Fanny DeWolf could be *proud* of her husband in his heroic death.[1]

Porter had collected DeWolf's possessions, including several unopened letters from Fanny that had arrived since the battle. He promised to send the collection to her upon his return to Bismarck at the end of the campaign. He concluded the letter with an expression of his heartfelt sympathies and signed it "H.R. Porter, A.A. Surg. USA," dated "July 28, 1876," and headed "Camp on the mouth of the Big Horn River—Montana Territory."[2]

Just two days earlier, the *Far West* had finally reached General Terry's camp, located about a mile below old Fort Pease on the north bank of the Yellowstone River. Hardly had Porter disembarked from the steamer than Terry gave orders to move the camp again, this time farther down the Yellowstone to the bank opposite the mouth of Rosebud Creek. With each passing summer day, the water levels fell and jeopardized the movement of the steamers to the upper reaches of the rivers. The critical delivery of supplies, particularly rations and forage, greatly preoccupied Terry. The men and animals in his column required, on average, some 3,000 pounds of food and 14,500 pounds of grain (oats or corn) *per day*. Such a load strained the carrying capacity of wagons, especially over the rough terrain of the area. Clearly steamboats were the answer to the general's transportation needs. By relocating his base camp to within reach of the steamers, Terry could guarantee the feasibility, if not the success, of the continuing campaign.[3]

The Dakota column had worked in concert with Colonel Gibbon's Montana column since the middle of June. But these two prongs of General Sheridan's original three-prong assault on the Sioux had yet to reckon with the third prong, that of Brigadier General George Crook and his column from Wyoming. On July 12, couriers from Terry reached Crook's camp with dispatches describing the Custer disaster at the Little Big Horn. Crook returned those couriers with news from the south. Both generals expressed their intent to coordinate, but both also awaited reinforcements then en route.

The first to arrive in Terry's camp was Lieutenant Colonel Elwell S. Otis and six companies of the Twenty-Second Infantry from Detroit, which were delivered by the steamer *Carroll*. Colonel Nelson A. Miles and six companies of the Fifth Infantry from Fort Leavenworth in the Department of the Missouri were close behind onboard the steamer *E. F. Durfee*. One hundred and fifty men and sixty-five horses destined to fill the ranks of the depleted Seventh Cavalry accompanied Miles.

Doctor Porter had bided his own time onboard the *Far West* as it steamed against the currents of the Missouri and the Yellowstone on its return trip from Bismarck to Terry's camp. Standing on the boat's deck on July 20, when it passed the *Josephine* and a cargo of discharged soldiers, Porter took note of the stone-faced cavalrymen on that boat's deck, men who had had enough of soldiering and were eager to return home. It was a brief glimpse into the dangerously poor state of morale that he would soon encounter at the Yellowstone camp.

General Terry had hoped these several weeks in camp would allow his men to recover physically and psychologically from the exhaustion and trauma of the June battles against the Sioux and Northern Cheyenne. The reprieve would also permit the arrival of reinforcements and supplies. As it happened, however, the weeks of delay had a detrimental effect. Feelings of fear, doubt, and guilt lingered in the camp as the men of the Seventh Cavalry brooded over the deaths of nearly half of their comrades and recalled the grisly aftermath of battle. It was an outcome that continued to bewilder and to challenge conventional explanations. Their own ordeal—nearly three days of "exhaustion, thirst, terror and death" followed by the work of burying over two hundred "decaying, rotting corpses" and enduring a physically grueling evacuation of the wounded—continued to haunt their thoughts and dreams. Their collective memory conjured up visions of many thousands of fierce, well-armed, sharpshooting Indians who had exacted a stunning toll on a superb regiment. In fireside discussions the men tended to amplify the odds they had faced as a way to make sense of the troubling defeat. But such exaggerations could not dispel the irrational gnaw of fear. And every man knew that such emotions were not soldierly.[4]

Demoralization pervaded Terry's camp. Contrary to his best intentions, the men were not rested or at all well. They were not officially ill, so there was little that Porter or any of the other surgeons could do to ease their anxiety. Some found palliation in whiskey purchased from traders who occasionally arrived in small skiffs from Bozeman to the west. Captain Thomas Weir of the Seventh Cavalry was a frequent customer. In the aftermath of Little Big Horn, with the discovery of the stripped and often mutilated corpses of Custer and his men, Weir had slipped into a despondency deep enough to lead him to drink in grave excess. Over Major Reno's objections, the captain had attempted to ride to Custer's aid but was repulsed by charging Indians. Guilt over his failure and his anger at Reno possessed him for the rest of the campaign and ultimately the remaining few months of his life.[5]

One week before Porter's return to the Yellowstone, with the medical care of Terry's and Gibbon's troops in the hands of an assistant surgeon, Captain John W. Williams, and five other physicians, despair claimed a life. At daybreak on July 19, Captain Lewis Thompson of the Second Cavalry in Colonel Gibbon's command shot himself in the heart. Friends of the officer knew of the chronic "neuralgia and nervous prostration" from which he suffered, derived largely from his time spent in Virginia's Libby Prison during the Civil War. But as a member of the Second Cavalry under Major Eugene M. Baker, Thompson also had participated in the punitive action taken against Piegan Indians in northern Montana, where on January 23, 1870, Baker obliterated a Piegan village, killing some 173 men, women, and children. In the summer heat and idleness of Terry's camp on the Yellowstone, among too many men with strained nerves, Captain Thompson seemed unable to keep his painful memories and personal demons at bay. His suicide was still reverberating through the camp when Porter arrived seven days later.[6]

By the end of July, doctors began to suspect that the lassitude, loss of appetite, and general irritability of many men in Terry's camp stemmed from more than idleness and sadness. There were other, plainly physical symptoms common to too many: swollen joints, easy bruising, and visible bleeding. Soon it became apparent that compounding the mental demoralization of the command was the physical debilitation deriving from a terribly simple factor: diet. For too long the men had subsisted on the basic army ration of bacon, hard tack, and coffee. Too seldom did they have fresh meat and almost rarely did they consume fresh or dried vegetables or fruit. Much to the chagrin of the doctors, all of whom were well aware of the hazards of the regular campaign diet, scurvy had settled in among the soldiers. Thirty-five to forty men were debilitated at a time, some too weak and uncomfortable to walk. The surgeons' supplies of antiscorbutics—lime juice, pickles, dried fruits, and vegetables—were quickly depleted. Fresh supplies arriving by boat were unpredictable. Men scoured the landscape for wild onions, watercress, and berries. Even the juice of the prickly pear cactus, which could be flavored with whiskey, provided a meager dose of much-needed vitamin C.[7]

Newspaper correspondent James J. O'Kelly of the *New York Herald* arrived by steamer at Terry's camp on August 1 to cover the next phase of the continuing campaign, and it did not take him long to editorialize on the preventable sickness he observed: "No attempt was made by the Commissary Department to send the troops vegetables, although the river affords every facility. During the campaign they have had to subsist chiefly on pork and crackers, a diet that would, in a short time, make havoc with the stomach of an ostrich."[8]

For all of Terry's efforts to amass sufficient supplies for the continuation of the expedition, this simple dietary oversight compromised the health of his men. The challenge was to have not only adequate quantities of rations but also healthy rations. The longer the command remained in the field, the more adverse were the effects of passing time. On August 2, twenty soldiers, incapacitated by illness, headed down the Yellowstone onboard the *Carroll* bound for Fort Abraham Lincoln. There seemed to be no stopping the attrition in the command.

Morale rose somewhat with the arrival of healthy soldiers. The *Carroll* delivered the Twenty-Second Infantry on August 1, and the *E. F. Durfee* arrived the next day loaded with Colonel Nelson A. Miles's Fifth Infantry plus 150 fresh cavalry recruits. The *Josephine* soon followed with supplies, ordnance, and sixty-four horses.[9] Along with able bodies, the steamers also brought useful intelligence. Indians firing from near the Powder River depot had made that locale a "hot" passage for the steamboats. This news worried General Terry. Suddenly aware of the vulnerability of his vitally important supplies, he ordered Major Orlando Moore with three companies of infantry and two scouts to steam sixty-five miles downriver on the *Far West* to the depot, where supplies of fodder were stockpiled. Armaments onboard the boat included a Napoleon smoothbore cannon and a Gatling gun. Aware of the possibility of a confrontation with Indians, Terry also ordered Porter to accompany the soldiers.

Major Moore found seventy-five tons of oats sacked at the abandoned depot. Indians had rummaged the sacks and scattered the grain: they had no need for oats since their ponies were grass fed. Several rounds from the Napoleon cannon scattered the Indians who appeared on the horizon as the soldiers worked to bag and load the forage onto the steamboat. But a later altercation between lingering warriors and the two scouts with Moore's detail left one scout mortally wounded. Porter attempted to stop the bleeding in William Brockmeyer's chest, but the gunshot from close range had damaged major blood vessels. The scout died a few hours later and was buried at the depot. At the burial a lieutenant read from an inspirational booklet that had been in Brockmeyer's possession, then bundled it with a sprig of sage and a cottonwood leaf and sent it to the man's sister in the East. The civility of the ceremony touched many of the men. For Henry Porter, it was yet another death of a soldier under his care.[10]

With the arrival of the reinforcements and supplies, Terry again planned a departure from the Yellowstone. The pace of preparation was slow, in keeping with Terry's careful deliberations but much to the ire of other officers. First Lieutenant Frank Baldwin, adjutant to Colonel Miles's battalion, confessed his dismay in a letter to his wife: "This is miserable country nothing but sand and dust, if they would only move, and get through with this thing and let us out it would not be so tedious but we are doing nothing. There are 1750 fighting men here a force large enough to whip all the Sioux in the country if they will go at them and not get scart. . . . I cant begin to find language to express my disgust at the manner things are being run here. Slow is no name for it."[11]

The command finally moved out on August 8, forty-four days after Custer's annihilation at the Little Big Horn. The reorganized force numbered some 940 infantry; 730 cavalry; ten physicians; seventy-five Crow and Arikara scouts; forty provisional artillerymen for the Napoleons, Gatlings, and Rodmans; and 203 six-mule wagons, each laden with ammunition, rations, and forage.[12] At more than 1,600 officers and men, the force satisfied Terry's desire for offensive and defensive size. Others, however, registered dismay at the enormity of the military column. Outspoken Lieutenant Baldwin anticipated events to come in another letter: "I don't think there is any use of worrying about our getting into a fight with the Indians for I don't believe we will see an Indian during the 35 days we are expected to be out. We will probably move very slow and as we will be lumbered with an imence train it will impede our progress so that we will not be able to follow them after we find their camp, if we are in luck to do such a thing."[13]

The slow pace was made all the more intolerable by the blistering heat of the day, with temperatures reaching 109 degrees in the shade. The water along the way was alkaline and unhealthy. Mosquitoes tormented the men at night. Then the Montana latitude exhibited its unpredictability one evening by administering a fifty-degree drop in temperature, and the command awoke to threatening skies and chilly conditions. Cold air and the indications of rain almost justified some of the equipment transported in the wagons: wall tents, beds, bedding, kitchen furniture, and even carpets—all for the officers, of course. At the mature age of forty-nine, General Terry consistently attended to the comfort and well-being of his peers, even if such concerns compromised their ability to "whip the hostiles."[14]

Believing the Indians to be in camp at the base of the Big Horn Mountains, the column lumbered south thirty-six miles alongside Rosebud Creek. In the clear, cold morning air of August 10, scouts spied a large dust cloud some ten miles up the Rosebud. Cries of "Sioux" and shouted orders generated all manner of battle readiness. The column came alive with anticipation and purpose. Some men indulged in talk of revenge, while others simply wanted to see action or anything other than the deadly monotony they had endured in camp. Private Eugene Grant of the Seventh Infantry described the commotion: "The cavalry formed a line of battle, the infantry deployed as skirmishers on the bluffs, the artillery behind the cavalry. The wagon train was 'parked,' and we were ready for the savages."[15]

Binoculars trained on the dust cloud at last picked out an unexpected detail: a single rider had emerged, moving in the direction of Terry's column. When the rider waved a broad, white hat, thoughts of "hostiles" evaporated, but the man's identity remained puzzling. Finally Captain Benteen yelled to his troops on the skirmish line: "Three cheers for Buffalo Bill!"[16] The men enthusiastically complied.

Any disappointment some initially felt at not confronting Indians was tempered by the anticipation of seeing the famous Buffalo Bill Cody, already the hero of popular dime novels and an actor who played himself in melodramas about the Wild West. Cody had scouted for Custer in 1867, and in 1872 Custer and Cody had guided a successful buffalo-hunting excursion for the Grand Duke Alexis, son of Tsar Alexander II of Russia.

Eventually, everyone realized that it was Crook's column and not the Sioux that stirred the dust in the distance. As for the effort and energy that had gone into preparing for battle, Private Grant phrased it succinctly: "Too bad, all that martial array for nothing." In the deployment twelve of the new cavalry recruits had fallen from their horses, with two of them breaking a leg. Fresh recruits and inexperienced horses were among Terry's trying concerns.[17]

Forty-nine-year-old George Crook, commander of the Department of the Platte, had departed Fort Fetterman, Wyoming, on May 29 with his column, dubbed the "Big Horn and Yellowstone Expedition." At the head of the Rosebud, on June 17 he had fought the Sioux to a draw. Falling back to his base camp on Goose Creek near the Tongue River, Crook's command remained there for the next seven weeks, stewing over the failure of this battle and awaiting reinforcements and supplies. The location proved nearly idyllic, and the men spent their time hunting and fishing.[18]

On August 3, Colonel Wesley Merritt and the Fifth Cavalry arrived in camp, and two days later the reinforced command at last moved out. On August 10, when the Wyoming column encountered Terry's troops, the three prongs of General Sheridan's original plan had at last converged.

Terry wrote triumphantly to his sister: "My force united with General Crook's today about noon. We have together from 3100 to 3200 men, enough to whip all the Indians on the continent."[19] The military array indeed was impressive. Although the two generals largely agreed that the northern Indians had moved east from the Big Horn Mountains, their opinions diverged as to what to do next. Terry believed that the Indians would eventually cross the Yellowstone River and head north toward the British Possessions. Crook thought that many would simply move farther east toward the agencies. In fact, both were right. Nevertheless, they continued to believe that a very large body of Indians continued to roam the Yellowstone River countryside.

General Terry was justified in boasting of the size of the combined columns. Crook's force alone was immense, composed of 1,450 cavalrymen, 425 infantrymen, 230 Shoshone scouts, twenty Ute scouts, thirty civilians, and 350 pack mules.[20] Despite its formidable size, however, the command was an efficient and mobile force. Crook had made a science of mule packing during his time in Arizona Territory and held the strong conviction that mules afforded an Indian-fighting army the utmost mobility. His mules transported ammunition, medical supplies, rations, and little else. Soldiers carried weapons, accoutrements, a few personal items, and little more. There was not a single tent in the command. It would have been generous to call the general's campaign style Spartan.

The disparity between Crook's and Terry's columns was perhaps best represented by a single item: the Brussels carpet that covered the ground in Major Reno's wall tent. Privately Crook expressed disgust at the equipage in Terry's command, which was sure to hamper mobility. He confided to a friend, "We shall find no Indians while such a force sticks together."[21] But Terry soon adopted Crook's austere style, ordering that the hardiest of his mules be converted from wagon mules to pack mules carrying only the bare essentials. He stipulated that his men should bring no more than a blanket along with their standard military gear. His 203 wagons then transported everything else to the supply camp at the mouth of Rosebud Creek.

By all appearances, Terry's column was now ready to keep stride with Crook's men.

The events of subsequent days, however, proved otherwise. Lieutenant John Bourke, aide-de-camp to General Crook and a true soldier-scholar with a keen eye for detail and the talent to put it into words, described what he saw: "Terry's pack train was a burlesque: formed of mules freshly taken from the harness and with attendants rivaling animals in dumbness." He also noted that unruly mules were not the sole problem. Terry's column generally was "unwieldy, lacked cohesion and was spiritless to the point of demoralization." The heavy rains that started to fall on August 12 exacerbated these dysfunctions and caused many more. Marching over difficult terrain and at times in knee-deep mud exhausted both man and beast. The cavalrymen dismounted and walked their horses to ease the burden. Nevertheless, weakened horses in need of grain "played out" and were abandoned or had to be shot. Terry's newly recruited infantrymen became disabled by bleeding feet and swollen legs to the point where many lay down exhausted in the mud. To keep up the pace of the march, often only two miles an hour, many of the newcomers were conveyed on mules or carried on hastily made travois.[22]

What remained of the comfortable summer weather ended abruptly. Cold rain continued for days and nights, making conditions miserable. Fatigue from daytime marching through what newspaper correspondent John F. Finerty described as the "most adhesive mud on the American continent" evolved into utter exhaustion at night, when men, desperate for rest, slumped in mounds under the wet torrents.[23] As though mocking Terry's recent decision to forgo some conventional army supplies—tents, tarps, and overcoats—and adopt instead Crook's campaign austerity, the northern climate delivered four days and nights of wretched weather. Even the usually cheery campfires became victims of the rain—with no way to cook, men ate raw bacon and sodden hardtack. No fire also meant there was no coffee to warm their bodies and lift their spirits. Terry's decision to emulate Crook's style dealt another body blow to the morale of his men, putting them at risk for exposure. It was the beginning of a protracted nightmare for the medical staff.

On the fourth day of the columns' joint march, a young captain in the Twenty-Second Infantry suddenly dropped to the muddy ground and lay immobile. The surgeons in Terry's column, including Henry Porter, quickly came to his aid only to discover that he was paralyzed on his left side and unable to speak. They diagnosed a "severe attack of apoplexy"—a stroke—brought on by the arduous conditions of the march.[24] For days the officers had suffered the same exposure as the enlisted men, and now young Captain Archibald Goodloe paid a serious price. Once again the army faced the challenge of transporting the sick. As he had done before for the wounded of the Seventh Cavalry, Lieutenant Doane offered his services in constructing a litter. Within two hours the men had lifted Captain Goodloe—a paralyzed, mute, and undoubtedly frightened officer—onto the relatively comfortable device. The column soon moved again, still at the mercy of torrential rains.

Terry and Crook followed a faint Indian trail to the east, but on August 16 Terry decided to abandoned the current pursuit and instead march north to the supply camp at the confluence of the Powder and Yellowstone Rivers. Goodloe's misfortune clearly indicated the risks being undertaken, and some men needed to heal, especially those in Crook's column. Crook at first resisted the proposed holdup in the campaign but followed Terry's lead.

Exposure to the incessant rain and overexertion on the muddy trails may have precipitated Captain Goodloe's paralytic state. The adverse conditions also aggravated all manner of neuralgias and arthritis in infantrymen and cavalrymen alike. The troopers in the Seventh Cavalry ranged in age from seventeen to forty-nine, with the average being a youthful twenty-five. Young and old alike claimed back and joint pains, which was not surprising since the men jolted along daily for long hours on the army-issued McClellan saddles, lightweight and durable but "cursed as being only slightly softer than a granite boulder." Adding to the impact of the hard saddle was the weight of the standard carbine—Springfield Model 1873—at 7.9 pounds. Men carried it "on the right side suspended on a broad leather strap that rested on the left shoulder where most of the carbine's weight was centered." Together these two pieces of essential cavalry equipment contributed to back, spine, and disc problems, in addition to pain. The cold, wet weather of the mid-August march accentuated these degenerative aches, or perhaps the weather merely deprived the men of usual ways to distract themselves from their chronic "neuralgias." Even the isolated contusion, trauma most often caused by a horse or mule kick, flared in the foul weather and increased the level of physical discomfort.[25]

As Porter and all of the doctors accompanying Terry and Crook realized, an army on the march faced many tribulations, from mental and physical stress, to broken bones, to prostrations like Goodloe's apoplexy. But of all the maladies plaguing soldiers on campaign, no ailment may have been as widespread and debilitating as diarrhea. Montana's occasional foul weather provided several explanations for the indisposition. Since the beginning of the campaign, men had suffered sporadically from the purgative effects of drinking alkaline water, often experiencing bouts of cramping and diarrhea; Doctor Lord had experienced such symptoms just before the Battle of the Little Big Horn. But as cases of diarrhea multiplied, the surgeons began to suspect that there was more than alkaline contamination in the drinking water. The muddy conditions in which some 3,200 men were living and marching together during several days greatly increased the odds of fecal contamination. The overly saturated ground had lost its absorbent property, and water and solid matter ran over and spilled everywhere. Streams of water then dispersed the contaminants indiscriminately. Whenever a soldier rinsed his hands or in any way ingested local water, he risked infection. Had the rains not doused the campfires, men might have been able to boil away most impurities.

Bacteria such as salmonella and shigella in the water also would have caused intestinal cramping and diarrhea. Surgeons of the day as yet had no knowledge of microscopic bacteria, but they certainly understood that impure water and unhygienic living conditions caused both diarrhea and dysentery. Since the Civil War, doctors had distinguished between diarrhea and dysentery: cramping, and sometimes blood, accompanied the latter.[26] By all accounts, Henry Porter and other surgeons with the columns were treating both diarrhea and dysentery in the ranks, and the drug of choice for both conditions was camphorated opium tincture, otherwise known as paregoric. Unlike laudanum—a simple tincture of opium—paregoric was a mixture of benzoic acid, camphor, and glycerin flavored with anise oil, which gave it a licorice-like taste. Like laudanum it was a narcotic, but paregoric contained much less opium, thus having less of the addictive effect that had come to distinguish laudanum. The opiate worked to stop normal peristalsis in the intestine, calming the cramping and arresting the diarrhea. The exhausted patient was hardly cured, yet he at least gained a period of reprieve from the uncomfortable symptoms. Surgeons also administered a dose of chloral hydrate to some, guaranteeing a night of much needed sleep.[27] Eventually officers issued formal orders not to drink the water.

In a war of intimidation and dominance, numbers carried valuable weight. But maintaining Terry's and Crook's combined columns came with a heavy cost. Unwieldy size compromised maneuverability and speed. A sizable force required vast stockpiles of supplies. Shortages of rations and of essential nutrition risked malnutrition and scurvy. In a letter to his wife, 2nd Lieutenant Charles Roe of the Second Cavalry explained the predicament: "When we are out on the march, the column stretches about five miles long—it is a big army—the largest ever in an Indian country. The Sioux will not stand and fight it. The bird has flown now at any rate. We are only marching now, I think, for effect." The resignation expressed in Roe's letter was mild compared to the sarcasm voiced in a report written by newspaper correspondent Joseph Wasson: "All this big outfit needs to perfect it is half a dozen brass bands and [*New York*] *Herald* correspondents. Perhaps [Editor] James Gorden Bennett's fleet of yachts, if necessary." As to the meeting of the columns, Wasson echoed the sentiment circulating in Crook's command: "the junction of these forces . . . came about accidentally, and, as it now appears, very unfortunately." Crook was done with delays and let it be known in his command that he intended to cut loose from the joint columns just as soon as he received the rations and supplies so generously promised by Terry. The general then could regain his desired independence and march at a Roman pace, unencumbered by equipage, tedious thoughts of supplies, and any compromise resulting from inexperience.[28]

On August 23, the surgeons of the combined medical staffs took stock of the enlisted men and determined that many should be sent to hospitals at Fort Buford and Fort Abraham Lincoln. Thirty-four incapacitated men from Crook's column, fourteen with "acute Dysentery and Diarrhea," boarded the *Far West;* another twenty-one men, including two who had gone insane, headed for Omaha Barracks; and medical examiners ordered ten "incapacitated" soldiers of the Fifth Cavalry onto the boat as well. In some cases, especially those involving issues of sanity, there was no sure way for surgeons to determine if a soldier was genuinely ill or just "shamming" in an attempt to be released from the monotony of raw bacon, jaw-breaking hardtack, contaminated water, shelterless nights, interminable rain, and unyielding mud. Thirteen dollars a month may not have compensated for such conditions. Among the legitimate patients onboard the steamer was Captain Goodloe. The fact that the officer could sit up indicated a marked improvement in his condition, though he was still paralyzed on his right side and entirely unable to speak. Many in Terry's column had considered Private Mike Madden to be one of the unluckiest among the wounded in the summer campaign. But the future for a man with an amputated leg was much more promising than that which awaited Captain Goodloe if his condition remained permanent.[29]

From the appearance of the sky on August 23, all those in the Powder River camp feared they were in for an especially difficult night. Nature delivered another dramatic storm, with torrential rain, a cold north wind, thunder, and lightning. Men huddled in groups, trying to share body heat. Some lay sleeping on ground that gradually deteriorated into mud holes. The lightning and claps of thunder spooked the horses and mules, which pulled their picket pins from the saturated ground and ran amok. Newspaper correspondent John Finerty thought it was enough to ward off water and deafening peals of thunder as he lay in a makeshift bedroll on the ground. But when something seemingly akin to the weight of an elephant walked over him, his unleashed fury inspired him to deliver the beast a punch with his carbine: "by the vigorous kick which it gave my saddle in return, I became aware of the presence of a scared pack-mule." Finerty eventually fell asleep but awoke later "to find water running over, under, and all around me. To get up was useless, so I lay and soaked in my clothes until morning came, gray, cold and cheerless." He later claimed that the "experience of that night was the nearest approach to hell upon earth." The distress of Lieutenant Colonel Eugene Carr of the Fifth Cavalry was so great during the night that he even entertained an inconceivable envy for the body of a dead Indian lying nearby on a traditional elevated scaffold: "I got so depressed I began to think I would like to change places with the old dead Indian in the tree who had braved the storms of Montana for many years with his three blankets and robes." As dawn grayed the night sky, semi-drowned men trudged through the mud toward early morning campfires, where cups of hot coffee provided some relief from their misery.[30]

It was correspondent James O'Kelly of the *New York Herald* who put into words what the army surgeons could only think in private. "The health of the troops has suffered severely since the union of Terry's and Crook's columns," he began his dispatch. From there he accused Crook of adhering blindly to the theory that to fight Indians, one must live like them, abandoning shelter tents and even all cooking utensils except for a tin cup. That general's influence on the "good-natured" Terry was, by O'Kelly's account, beyond regrettable: "the mere fact that soldiers sleep in the rain and get dysentery and rhumatism will not make them better Indian fighters." O'Kelly pressed for greater common sense: "general and soldiers, abandoning theatrical campaigning, will sleep under canvas and cook their food, convinced that sound health and a well-ordered stomach are no obstacles to the rapid marching of an army."[31] None of the concerned surgeons of the medical staff could have said it better. For every conflict, tactic, and occasion for glory—the focus of generals—there were wounds, broken bones, and disease—the concerns of surgeons.

General Terry fulfilled his pledge of supplies for General Crook's men on the morning of August 23. There was much to be provided, and only the promised tobacco was wanting, obliging soldiers to scrounge for alternatives. With receipt of the supplies, Crook returned to the trail the next day. Fighting mud with every step, his men finally submitted and made camp after only nine miles. Terry's troops fared somewhat better when they set off the following day in clear weather. Mud and rivers swollen from the rains impeded the progress of infantry, cavalry, and the wagon train, carrying three weeks of supplies. After only seventeen miles, the fatigued column established camp.

While Terry's and Crook's commands were marching up the Powder River, the steamer *Carroll* set off down the Yellowstone, transporting the sick and wounded destined for hospitals at Fort Buford, Fort Abraham Lincoln, and Omaha Barracks. The vessel met the steamers *Josephine* and *Yellowstone* coming upriver and carrying critical news about increasing numbers of Indians seen at Glendive Creek, fifty miles downriver. A courier relayed this news overland to Terry, who feared the Sioux would attempt to cross the Yellowstone and find sanctuary in the Big Open, that vast expanse of eastern Montana generally bounded by the Yellowstone to the south, the Missouri to the north, and the Musselshell to the west. It was the prime range for the northern buffalo to the very last.

While Crook headed east in search of the Sioux he felt certain were traveling back toward the agencies, Terry realized that his season of campaigning had come to an end. He left troops to picket the Yellowstone and establish a cantonment, or temporary quarters, at the mouth of the Tongue River. Then on September 5 he issued the official order to end the "Expedition against hostile Sioux." In the chill and mist of September 6, the columns separated. Surgeon Holmes Paulding with Gibbon's troops recorded in his diary on September 6: "'The Expedition against hostile Sioux' died a natural death & we all started on our various homeward trails. Ours is 446 miles long."[32]

Terry directed Reno and the Seventh Cavalry toward Wolf Point, an Indian agency along the Missouri River, where agents recently had observed as many as 150 Indians crossing to the north side of the river. Before setting out, the major took the occasion to lessen his load somewhat by culling from the ranks those soldiers no longer able to ride. These men went aboard the *Far West* for delivery to Fort Abraham Lincoln.

Standing by the gangplank, Captain Grant Marsh easily recognized the bone-deep weariness in the men and mules loading on to his steamboat. The soldiers looked thin, even gaunt, weakened from the effects of diarrhea and dysentery or the pains of rheumatism. They needed rest and nutritional fortification, neither of which could be provided in the field. Also onboard was the familiar figure of Surgeon Porter, detailed by Reno to minister to the sick men during the journey.[33]

This was a pleasant reunion of sorts for the steamer captain and the surgeon, their mutual respect established in July during the evacuation of the wounded survivors of the Little Big Horn. Few river runs would ever again compare with that trip in speed of travel and overall medical success, and of that Marsh and Porter could be equally proud. Now paired once again at the termination of the campaign, the two set to work with an ease that comes from familiarity. Both were intent on the same goal: the comfort of the patients. Captain Marsh realistically anticipated bumps and collisions with snags and sandbars during the trip ahead because the season was late and water levels low. But Porter would be less concerned about jolts to his patients since none were wounded or at risk of hemorrhaging. This time the soldiers onboard the *Far West* suffered from debilitations, usually completely preventable, about which men were reluctant to speak and assuredly would not choose to incorporate into their Indian Wars reminiscences.

But these were not shameful discomforts either. Most knew that such afflictions could be life threatening. In the Union Army during the Civil War, some 37,000 men died from diarrhea and dysentery, both acute and chronic. Surgeons were not yet armed with an understanding of intestinal microbes or germs, and Porter could only try to mitigate the symptoms and discomfort. His regimen included fortifying his patients with boiled beef stock, nutritious and safe because of the boiling process. Where necessary he would administer paregoric to slow the action of the cramping bowel. The drug was always effective but not without some risk of addiction. It was regrettable to relieve the symptom of one disease in a patient only to create a new and far more insidious disability through opium addiction, which became known as the "old soldier's disease." Because morphine and opium were the only effective painkillers known to medicine at the time, the odds of developing a drug addiction were dangerously high. But when Porter weighed that possibility against fatal dehydration—the prime risk of diarrhea—he had no choice but to save lives by any means.[34]

Many other soldiers on the *Far West* were broken down from the aches and pains of rheumatism, limiting their level of activity in the field. Some never wished to ride a horse again. Porter banked on the physical rest afforded the men for the duration of the trip to begin to ease their discomfort. But also aware of the extent to which scurvy had infiltrated Terry's camp, Porter suspected that many soldiers suffered from scurvy-induced bleeding into joints and muscles.[35] For them he prescribed eating anything containing vitamin C. As a last resort, there was always a dose of medicinal whiskey to ease any pain. Many of the patients seem to have preferred this measure above the others.

As the boat set off on September 10, a floating hospital whose purpose was to evacuate soldiers to the care of a military hospital, Porter no doubt felt less anxious than he had on the earlier evacuation but still regretful about his current charges. He would administer to them throughout the trip and, with luck, deliver most in some degree of recovery. Their disabilities, which had been avoidable, were curable. Even so, some of these men would be discharged, no doubt a desirable fate in the minds of many of those who had survived the Battle of the Little Big Horn.[36]

10

Afterlife of a Campaign

Soldiers mustered into the army; later they were *discharged,* honorably or not. Civilian surgeons signed *contracts* with the army; in time their contracts were *annulled.* There were no qualifiers for annulment. A contract surgeon departed from the army with no possible formal mention of honor.

The U.S. Army officially annulled its contract with Henry Porter on September 30, 1876, "the services of Dr. Porter being no longer required." The "Expedition against hostile Sioux," both costly and as yet nearly barren of results, reflected poorly on the army in the eyes of Congress and the nation. In 1874, Congress had rescinded its former restriction on the number of contract surgeons the army could hire, but it never fully reconciled itself to the army's need for these men. And as always, it communicated its displeasures fiscally. Surgeon General Joseph K. Barnes, constrained by fluctuating appropriations to the army's Medical Department, was barely able to meet the medical needs of the 239 posts spread throughout the country as well as of the numerous military deployments in the field.[1]

Hiring civilian surgeons on contract had given Barnes a flexible manpower solution that was especially useful in light of the 1876 congressional reduction of the number of authorized *commissioned* assistant surgeons from 150 to 125.[2] Contract surgeons filled the gaps and met the military's immediate and often changing needs, both of which were far better known to the surgeon general than to members of Congress. Nevertheless, legislators stubbornly continued to alter the number of contract surgeons employed by the army. Barnes could only let his medical directors in the various departments know which way the congressional winds were blowing. They were rarely favorable.

The medical director of the Department of Dakota, Lieutenant Colonel and Surgeon William J. Sloan, had contracted with Porter on May 15, 1876, "to perform the duties of a medical officer" at $125 a month for the duration of the "Expedition against hostile Sioux."[3] Roughly four and a half months later, Sloan dutifully informed the surgeon of the annulment of his contract. The dismissal of Porter helped the army meet a budget set by Congress; it is unclear, however, whether it suited the army's needs.

Porter's performance during the summer campaign with the Seventh Cavalry and General Terry's Dakota column was praiseworthy. Sloan reported to the surgeon general that "Acting Assistant Surgeon Porter discharged his duties during the late Sioux campaign to my entire satisfaction, and in a manner to elicit the approbation of all with whom he served." The chief medical officer of the expedition, Captain Williams, who had witnessed the location of the field hospital serving Reno's command on the hilltop, summed up Porter's success: "Dr. Porter deserves the highest praise for skill and courage under the most trying circumstances." Both official commendations were filed in the Surgeon General's Office at the War Department. They complemented Crook's written praise for the service Porter rendered during his first contract in Arizona Territory in 1872.[4]

Less formally, officers of the Seventh Cavalry also offered words of praise for Porter's performance in the Battle of the Little Big Horn. Major Reno delivered only a succinct statement: "I have never known a man to act a braver part."[5] Captain Benteen complimented the surgeon more profusely: "the stout heart and nervy skilful hand of Dr. Porter (the only surgeon of the three of the command that hadn't been killed), was equal to the occasion." Benteen placed him in a category of one: "I know of no doctor in the regular corps who would have performed the work which Dr. Porter did, with his small force of assistants; don't think there was or is one in the army." On another occasion the captain again lauded Porter's performance: "There was no nonsense, no gush about him, only just a strict attention to duty, and as modest about it as a girl in her teens."[6]

Despite his illustrious service and regardless of any desire to continue with the army, Porter's contract was annulled, and he returned to civilian life. Yet it was a short journey, a mere four miles, between Fort Abraham Lincoln and Porter's chosen city of residence.

Bruised by the bankruptcy of the Northern Pacific Railroad and the subsequent nationwide panic of 1873, the city of Bismarck waited out the bust years of economic depression. It continued as a busy port for steamboat traffic, as the western-most stop (if temporary) on the Northern Pacific, as the urban center closest to Fort Abraham Lincoln, and as the stagecoach terminus for gold seekers bound for Deadwood in the Black Hills. The city had evolved from a rough-and-tumble tent camp primarily serving railroad workers and now claimed a population of nearly 2,000 people, most of whom held their breath while the Northern Pacific reorganized itself. Residents exhaled a collective sigh when the railroad at last boasted earnings over expenditures, and in the fall of 1876, Bismarck once again held much promise for its people and investors. But most realized that success hinged on the railroad encouraging travelers and settlers to come and investigate the remote Dakota Territory despite its "far away sound," as one historian put it.[7]

Henry Porter returned to Bismarck just as its recovery had begun, and it was another two years before the economic boom soared. The city's population then supported the medical practice of Doctor Benjamin Franklin Slaughter, Bismarck's first full-time physician.[8]

Porter expected that as the Northern Pacific regained its financial footing, it would draw in workers, families, and investors, swelling the population to the point where it could easily support the practice of a second doctor. Porter's transition from army contract surgeon to civilian physician appeared smoothly greased by the inevitability of westward expansion, fueled by and manifested in the Northern Pacific Railroad.

Porter fully intended to hang his professional shingle in Bismarck, but first there were items of business related to the late summer campaign that he needed to address. Awaiting his return to Fort Abraham Lincoln around September 12 was another letter from Fanny DeWolf. On September 14 Porter responded to her many questions, one of which concerned her husband's remains. "Next spring," he wrote, "there will probably be an effort made to get the remains of the officers if so his body will of course be sent to you." In the meantime Fanny would soon receive her husband's personal possessions: a diary, unopened letters from her, a watch, a pocketbook containing ten dollars, a pillow, and an overcoat and clothing. Porter closed his letter with a personal request: "If you have a photograph of the Doctor to spare I should prize it very highly."[9] In the death of James DeWolf, he had lost both a colleague and friend.

Over the course of the fall months, Porter also learned of the status of the patients he had cared for on the hilltop at the Little Big Horn. It was a relief to hear that Private Madden had been discharged from the Fort Lincoln hospital on September 13. Although the stump of his amputated leg had been in an unhealthy condition when he arrived in early July, he had not succumbed to infection.[10] Two other soldiers were less fortunate. Private David Cooney, wounded in the right hip, probably from a bullet on June 26, died on July 20 of pyemia, or infection in the bloodstream. Private Frank Braun expired on October 4. During surgery just weeks earlier, surgeons probed his infected femur and extracted foreign matter, most likely dragged in with the original bullet. That invisible foe—

infection—could still outwit even the best surgeon's skill. Fifty-nine men had been wounded during the fights in the timber and on the hilltop on June 25 and 26. It was in large measure thanks to Henry Porter that only six of them (Lell, George, King, Bennett, Cooney, and Braun) died in the aftermath of the battle.[11]

Three months after Porter's contract annulment, as it struggled to deal with the contending demands of the various regiments serving in the Department of Dakota, the army suddenly contacted the doctor on December 2, 1876, and offered yet another contract. It would be Porter's fifth. Medical Director Sloan already had written to the surgeon general requesting permission to establish the agreement: "Owing to complications and wants not anticipated, there has been a constant demand for medical officers." The summer campaign against the Sioux had evolved into several subsequent efforts: "the whole force of Sitting Bull has been encountered and whipped twice between [Fort] Buford and Tongue River." In addition, explained Sloan: "A second expedition, the destination of which was kept secret, was organized at Fort A. Lincoln, commanded by General Terry and composed of twelve hundred (1200) cavalry and three (3) companies of infantry." Terry's large show of force was necessary in order to fulfill the instructions given by General Sheridan to divest the Indians living on the Standing Rock and Cheyenne Agencies of their firearms and ponies. "A Sioux on foot is a Sioux no longer," argued Sheridan. Even into the fall, troops along the Missouri River remained active. But as winter approached, most commands were ordered into quarters at their respective posts.[12]

Among the twenty-four posts for which Sloan provided medical staff and care was Camp Hancock in Bismarck. Porter's residency there, merely city blocks away from Hancock, made him an attractive candidate to oversee the health of the small infantry garrison. On December 2 Sloan drew up a proposed contract with Porter to provide medical services at Camp Hancock for sixty dollars a month.[13]

The deep winter months in Dakota Territory were notoriously frigid, almost as cold as the attitude legislators maintained toward the army and its many departments. Congress had sharply reduced the military's appropriations for the year 1877, in fact never appropriating for the army that year. This tactic derived, in part, from the determination of southern congressmen to force the removal of occupation forces from their states entirely. They exercised a point of leverage in their effort to regain greater postwar independence, leverage felt throughout the military institution, including its medical department. Caught in the congressional squeeze, Surgeon General Barnes fired off a directive in February 1877 to each of his department medical directors, ordering them to reduce the number of contract surgeons in their employment. He advised them instead to "rely on local physicians . . . employed by the visit."[14]

It turned out to be Porter's shortest stint yet with the army. On February 28, 1877, after employing the civilian surgeon for only two months, Sloan carried out his instructions from Washington: "I have the honor to report that I have this day annulled the contract with Acting Assistant Surgeon H. R. Porter, at Camp Hancock, on account of insufficient appropriation of money for the payment of Contract Surgeons." Congressional austerity and anti-army sentiment led to the termination of Porter's fifth contract, but it did not quite put him out of work. "Dr. Porter will continue to furnish medical attendance to the troops stationed at Camp Hancock," Sloan stated, "and will be responsible for the medical and Hospital property at that station." While he had indeed reduced the number of contract surgeons, Sloan had also fulfilled the second recommendation in the surgeon general's directive by relying on the services of a local physician. Porter endured the disruption of the annulment, but he maintained his army employment thanks to the medical director's clever maneuvering.[15]

With five army contracts in five years, 1872–77, some would have considered Porter fortunate to maintain an income during the decade's economic bust. But as the Indian Wars were inherently unpredictable, so too were the army's demands for resources, human and otherwise. The military's dealings with its civilian employees, including wagon masters, teamsters, guides, interpreters, and contract surgeons—in short, the ones who seemed the last to be hired and the first to be fired—furnished early signals of any change in its plans. For a young surgeon who was still a bachelor, this unpredictability translated into opportunity and adventure. But somewhere in the fits and starts of this ad hoc life, opportunity of another sort emerged. When Porter became a physician five years earlier, he had followed in the ancestral footsteps of three generations before him.[16] He broke with tradition, however, when he did not settle into a private practice, choosing instead to couple his medical training with other youthful interests. Serving the army as a contract surgeon satisfied his urge to travel and his enthusiasm for adventure. Now at this stage in his career, Porter was a prime candidate to take the army's medical exam and become a commissioned officer. This, in fact, was considered the height of ambition in 1867 by another contract surgeon, James P. Kimball, who aimed for the "honorable position of an officer in the United States Army," which he achieved.[17]

To guarantee that surgeons in the medical department remained an elite corps, the army held them to high standards, beginning with an extensive entrance examination that could last as long as six days. Demonstration of a proficiency in medicine was just a start. Questions also required of a candidate knowledge of science, math, literature, history, and classical languages. What is the cube root of 3.6? What were the principal Roman deities and their Greek counterparts? What is Newton's first law of motion? What is the chemistry involved in glassmaking? Surgeons who passed the exam drew heavily on a classical education in addition to their medical training. Army surgeons were reputed to be repositories of culture and knowledge. The lack of such a classical foundation proved to be an insurmountable barrier for many otherwise fine civilian surgeons.[18]

Henry Norton Porter had secured for his son a respectable education when he sent the sixteen-year-old Henry Renaldo to Whitestown Seminary in the village of Whitestown, three miles west of Utica, New York. There he was exposed to a three-year curriculum that included philosophy, algebra, astronomy, plane and spherical trigonometry, U.S. history, chemistry, civil engineering, botany, and geology.[19] Had Porter wanted to take the army's medical exam in 1877, he would have called upon his seminary lessons, hoping his memory served him well. As it was, however, he never took the exam. Five years serving the army may have prepared the surgeon for an officer's position, but those years had also exposed him to that intangible, alluring quality of the West: opportunity. Ultimately, Porter paid no heed to the army's exam and the incentive of a commission. Instead he turned his attention to the booming western economy and the proliferation of business ventures in Bismarck. It seems that medicine was not the goal in itself for the young surgeon, but a means to other equally interesting ends.

The winter of 1877 introduced Porter to his first civilian medical practice and also to a young, accomplished woman from Oberlin, Ohio, visiting her sister in Bismarck. On September 4, 1877, Henry Renaldo Porter and Charlotte Jane Viets were married at her parents' home in Oberlin. On January 8, 1878, a contented Porter wrote in response to a recent request from the surgeon general: "In answer to your letter of the 29th ult. asking if 'I would like to enter into contract as A.A. Surg. U.S.A.' I have the honor to state that I do not care to at present. I appreciate fully and thank you for the honor thus conferred." Porter had exchanged a life of erratic army contracts for one of stability and prosperity as he established a medical practice within the growing population of Bismarck. In time his medical reputation gained him entry into many organizations. He became the surgeon for the Northern Pacific Railroad, physician to the state penitentiary at Bismarck, county physician of Burleigh County, founder of the Missouri Valley Medical Society, and president of the Medical Society of North Dakota. A business-minded man, Porter was one of the founders of the First National Bank of Bismarck and one of the incorporators of the State Bank of Morton County in Mandan. He purchased 160 acres of prime land overlooking the city, fourteen lots in Bismarck just as the local economic boom began in the late 1870s, and a tract of land near Rock Creek in Washington, D.C., acting on a tip that the government planned to build a zoological garden in the vicinity.[20]

Some veterans like Porter were able to stow away their summer experiences of 1876. Their jobs were completed, their reputations intact. But the "Expedition against hostile Sioux," and especially the Battle of the Little Big Horn, so often called the "massacre," persisted at the center of a national debate. Famed Boston abolitionist Wendell Phillips questioned the depiction of the Custer battle and the unfair treatment of Indians in general: "What kind of war is it, where if we kill the enemy it is death; if he kills us it is a massacre?" Many in the East regarded the army as a "gang of cutthroats" and "butchers, rampaging around the West slaughtering peaceable Indians." To depict the Indian-fighting army as the "advance guard of civilization" to many easterners was morally repugnant. Of course, westerners saw it otherwise.[21]

Some who debated the army's role in the West often employed bombastic rhetoric and sensational imagery, generating a picture more worthy of a dime novel than of the actual conditions west of the Missouri. A rare authentic view was Colonel Gibbon's version of events, "Last Summer's Expedition against the Sioux and its Great Catastrophe," published in the *American Catholic Quarterly Review* in 1877. This instructive account provided riveting detail, although toward the end it exceeded mere description as Gibbon issued an appeal for justice for the "red man": "You cannot point to one single treaty with the Indians which has not at some time or other been violated by whites, and you can point to innumerable instances where the Indian has been most outrageously swindled by the agents of the government." The respected officer urged his readers to see the situation through Indian eyes, concluding, "And the great wonder is, not that we have had so many wars but that we have had so few."[22]

Beyond the debate about the treatment of Indians by whites and the role of the army in enforcing the government's expansionist policies, another controversy brewed over Custer and the soundness or selfishness of his military judgment at the Little Big Horn. At issue was whether he had gambled the lives of the men in his own battalion in a quest for personal glory. Responsibility for the disastrous outcome would ultimately have to hang on someone's neck. If the regiment's colonel, Samuel Davis Sturgis, had any say, that neck would belong to Custer.

Colonel Sturgis, a brigadier general of volunteers during the Civil War, was appointed commanding officer of the Seventh Cavalry in 1869. He was adept at wrangling administrative assignments and did not accompany his regiment as a field commander—that role was played by Custer. In Sturgis's eyes Custer had squandered the lives of more than 200 men at the Little Big Horn, including one uniquely precious life, the colonel's son, 2nd Lieutenant James G. Sturgis, Company M, serving with Custer's fighting battalion. Young Sturgis's body was never identified, but his bloodstained underclothing was later recovered at the site of the Indian village, leading some to believe that the lieutenant had died a horribly gruesome death as a captive during the evening of June 25.

By mid-July 1876, Sturgis made quite public his opinion of Custer, condemning him as "mad and reckless" and filled with "unholy ambition." He considered it nothing short of a crime to glorify the man. "If a monument is to be erected to General Custer, for God's sake let them hide it in some dark alley, or veil it, or put it anywhere where the bleeding hearts of the widows, orphans, fathers, and mothers of the men so uselessly sacrificed to Custer's ambition can never be wrung by the sight of it."[23]

The urge to assign responsibility for the disaster produced another kind of battleground. Opinions split into camps. Late in 1876, less than six months after the battle, Frederick Whittaker published his *Complete Life of Major General George Armstrong Custer,* written in part with information provided by Custer's widow, Elizabeth. The hastily composed book propelled the debate forward by placing the blame for Custer's death on Major Reno and Captain Benteen. Battle lines now and hereafter were clearly and publicly drawn.

Speculation about the role of Reno in the battle had peppered quiet conversations in army camps throughout the summer campaign. Some felt Custer betrayed the major by not coming to his aid in a timely fashion as promised. Others, especially Captain Weir, believed Reno's delay up on the hilltop essentially sacrificed the lieutenant colonel and his men to the Indians. Reno had argued his case cogently at every opportunity during the summer expedition and afterward. While his facts were convincing, his arrogant and abrupt manner did his cause a disservice. "Reno's self important rudeness makes him unbearable," Lieutenant Godfrey had penciled into his journal on August 16. "He thinks he can 'snip' everybody and comment on the orders from Genl Terry's Hdqurs., and insult the staff, so there is not one [on] the personal staff on speaking terms [with him]." Colonel Gibbon had even placed the major under arrest briefly for insubordination. First Lieutenant John Bourke, with Crook's column, also detected a sense of insecurity behind Reno's difficult manner and offered an analysis: "Reno saved, more by good luck than good management, the remnant of the Seventh Cavalry at the Custer Massacre. He saw enough at that fight to scare him for the rest of his life. He will never make a bold move for ten years to come."[24] Hard as it was to charge the major with specific wrongdoing during the battle, it was easy enough in the aftermath to identify his shortcomings.

Those in the military could debate the issue among themselves and yet somehow still live and work together without a resolution. Such was not the case for James O'Kelly of the *New York Herald*, who had spent many weeks with Terry's column covering the second phase of the campaign. By September 16, when O'Kelly filed his final dispatch, he had overheard enough conversations around countless campfires to be able to articulate the burning questions. He began that report by professing a lack of confidence in the army's official account of the battle and calling for an investigation under oath. In question was "whether the massacre . . . must be charged to rashness of the dead or prudence of the living." O'Kelly detected a general impression among the Seventh Cavalry survivors that "had a tougher fight been made in the [wooded] bottom, the Indians could not have overwhelmed Custer with their whole force." In his "charge" to the hilltop, Reno had succeeded in disengaging the Indians, a move that assuredly saved what remained of his battalion. Once joined by Benteen, the hilltop force numbered seven companies, enough strength to compel the correspondent to protest: "If seven companies, instead of halting upon a hill, had advanced at a gallop, to where the firing was heard, instead of halting an hour or two on the hill, they could have arrived in ample time to have cooperated with Custer. There was nothing to prevent them from doing so."[25]

Major Reno and his supporters claimed, however, that a lack of cartridges had forced them to wait for the arrival of the slow-moving pack train and the ammunition-laden mules. Moreover, the men wounded in the timber fight, the river crossing, and the ascent of the bluffs were no longer fit for battle, and to abandon them on the hilltop, even temporarily, constituted a risk met with great moral aversion.

O'Kelly's provocative questions, together with Whittaker's public allegations of Reno's "gross cowardice and neglect of duty," stirred debate for nearly two years. Finally Whittaker called for a formal investigation by the Military Committee of the House of Representatives, but Congress adjourned without taking up the matter. By now even more disappointed than Whittaker was Major Reno, who was determined to regain his good name. He forced the issue by writing directly to President Rutherford B. Hayes to request a formal court of inquiry. The proposal won the president's approval and the subsequent authorization of General William T. Sherman, commander of the army. At last Reno would be able to tell his side of the story and also bring to bear eyewitness accounts in support of his decisions and actions.[26]

Twenty-three witnesses were subpoenaed to appear and testify before the court of inquiry, convened at the Palmer House in Chicago on January 13, 1879. Of these men, fourteen were officers in the Seventh Cavalry and others included Gibbon, Edward Maguire of the Corps of Engineers, a captain in the Fifth Cavalry, and five civilians: two packers, an interpreter, a scout, and Henry Porter. By now Porter was fully immersed in a successful career in Bismarck, but once again the army called, this time requesting that he serve as a witness to the judgment, actions, and demeanor of Marcus Reno.

Joining Porter on the train departing from Saint Paul, Minnesota, bound for Chicago were Captain Benteen, Lieutenant Varnum, Captain McDougall, 1st Lieutenant George D. Wallace, and 1st Lieutenant Luther R. Hare, all of the Seventh Cavalry. It was January 12, and all six men were due at the military court the following day. A reporter from the *Chicago Times* caught up with them and posed some questions. Benteen never missed an opportunity to skewer Custer: "All the talk about Reno's being able to reinforce Custer is simply absurd. Custer himself is responsible for the Little Big Horn action, and it is an injustice to attribute the blame to anyone else." Benteen remained consistently disdainful of Custer throughout his life. Five years earlier, in 1874, Custer had published an account of

his soldiering exploits in *My Life on the Plains*. With a cynical dele-
tion of a single letter, Benteen sarcastically renamed the book "My
Lie on the Plains" as part of his ceaseless campaign to expose what
he considered to be the selfishness at the core of Custer's actions.
The same reporter then approached Doctor Porter, who rather than
follow Benteen's lead, admitted that "Reno could have gone to the
rescue of Custer, but as to the result he could not say. It might have
saved Custer or it might have added Reno's command to the lost."
The newspaperman also learned from Porter that while the major
had been nominally in charge on the hilltop, it was Benteen who
had been the real, inspiring leader. And for the record, there indeed
had been animosity and jealousy between Reno and Custer. Not to
be entirely outscooped, another reporter, this one from the *St. Paul
Globe*, asked a blunt question: "Do you think the charge of cowardice will be proved?" Porter answered cautiously, "Well I can hardly
tell." But in the next breath the surgeon exposed his hand: "There is
certainly ground for it." His natural candor was a reporter's dream
come true.[27]

The court convened on the appointed day. The officers of the
Seventh Cavalry were handsomely attired in full dress uniforms,
although they excluded their swords from the regalia. In attendance
was a crowd of spectators that increased daily until, by newspaper
accounts, the proceedings had to be moved to a "more commodi-
ous new room." Even so, "spectators crowded close to the witness
stand and the counsel's table" and stood "against the walls and filled
the doors."[28] The Battle of the Little Big Horn had raised curiosity
and suspicion in the public's mind since the morning the very first
"Massacred!" headline had appeared in a newspaper. The moment
of truth was finally at hand, or so everyone believed, and curious
citizens wanted to hear the verdict delivered.

After ten days of various testimonies, the court recorder called
witness Henry Porter to the stand. The reporter for the *Pioneer Press*
of Saint Paul and Minneapolis took note of the doctor's appearance:

"The next witness was D. H. R. Porter, of Bismarck, a gentleman by the way, who rejoiced in a sandy, tortoise-shell complexion, Peruvian blonde hair, and a military mustache. He has a peculiar way of biting his words off short, which caused not a little consternation among the reporters."[29] Despite this peculiar habit of speech, possibly attributable to his Scottish background or New York upbringing, Porter impressed most people in the crowded room quite favorably. A reporter from the *Rome (New York) Citizen* was taken with the surgeon's congenial appearance: "Dr. P is a pronounced blonde, with a golden mustache, and like most of the other parties connected with the investigation he looks out on nature out of a pair of blue eyes. Taking him for all in all, he appears to be a very agreeable sort of physician, one who would make it almost a pleasure to have a leg sawed off through his instrumentality."[30]

Spectators and the press liked what they saw in Porter, and his testimony proceeded uneventfully until the court recorder put forth the question central to the inquiry: How did Major Reno's conduct impress the surgeon? Reno's counsel, Lyman D. Gilbert, erupted in objection: "He is a doctor of medicine, not of physiognomy. If he had felt Major Reno's pulse I would rely on his opinion, but feeling the pulse of his mind is an entirely different thing." The court sustained the objection. It was a momentary victory for the major, but both Reno and Gilbert strongly suspected that Porter would not refrain, if invited, from leveling some very candid criticism at his former battalion commander. The doctor had already referred to the confusion resulting from Reno's "charge" from the timber toward the bluffs and to the demoralization of the men on the hilltop, feeling as though "they had been whipped." And he had never hesitated to identify Benteen as the effective commanding officer, even though Reno ranked him. Porter's testimony would undoubtedly work at odds with the purpose of the defense, which aimed to depict the major's demeanor and actions as intentional, calculating, and commanding.[31]

On the following day, the first line of Reno's defense against Porter was intimidation. As the stenographer read the surgeon's testimony from the previous day, the *Pioneer Press* reporter noted the "cat-like way that Major Reno watched [Porter] to better stare him out of countenance." Reno even "moved his chair close alongside" Porter's witness chair, but the doctor remained unperturbed. The recorder then resumed his line of questioning, again inquiring if the major's conduct in the timber and on the retreat was "as such as to inspire his men with courage and bravery, or the contrary?" Gilbert again objected to the question: "I should have great respect for any officer's opinion in a point like this, but I must confess that a medical gentleman seems to be better qualified to prescribe medicine than opinions in military affairs." The court overruled this objection and requested that the witness proceed. Porter answered thoughtfully: "I did not see anything particularly heroic in his conduct, but I thought it was the reverse. He seemed a little embarrassed I thought. The bullets were flying around pretty thick, and it seemed to me he did not exactly know whether he had better stay there or get out. That was my impression at the time."[32]

In his cross-examination Gilbert tried another tack, this time directed at Porter's state of mind: "Doctor, were you not frightened at any time, so that your judgment might have been impaired?" "No, sir," Porter responded. Gilbert pressed his point: "Were you not, doctor, in point of fact not being a military man, actually so frightened that you were not capable of judging what was going on in your vicinity?" Recalling the moment in the timber when he was administering laudanum to a mortally wounded soldier, Porter admitted to feeling some fear: "When I found myself cut off from the men, and without a horse, then I was frightened." So honest and plausible was his answer that most in the room realized they too would have felt similarly in such circumstances. It was not an admission of weakness. But Gilbert kept alive his line of questioning, intent upon demonstrating that Porter's fright compromised his ability to grasp the meaning of the actions of those around him during the fighting and ultimately impaired his judgment of all things military. But the sturdy and resolute surgeon refused to yield. Only when the court recorder resumed his turn at questioning did Porter elaborate on what had made him "excited" in the timber: "I found myself without a horse and without arms, the soldiers retreating and leaving me and a number of Indians between them and myself. Under these circumstances I felt a trifle shook up." It was a confession of sorts, and his answer suggested that he had experienced a degree of agitation that indeed might have interfered with his judgment. Porter then retired from the witness chair, no worse for wear from Gilbert's attempt to discredit him as a frightened civilian. He had answered forthrightly and accurately under oath.

Four days later, on January 28, the *Pioneer Press* published an editorial on the proceedings of the inquiry. Its author, the reporter present throughout the event, highlighted details in order to offset the general tedium of the testimony, but as a result depicted many witnesses with overly broad brush strokes. In this manner Doctor Porter became known as the "frightened sawbones" who "confesses his fright with such charming naiveté" and is "probably fervently praying that he might never see a gun again." Porter seemed to intrigue the reporter both as a reliable and unreliable witness: "The only witness who appears to have discerned physiognomical marks of cowardice [on Reno] is this doctor, who was not a soldier and was evidently very far gone with fright himself." He nonetheless managed to complement Porter, implicitly praising the doctor's candor in contrast to that of the "military men [who] either evade the question [about Reno] as irrelevant or say frankly that Reno's conduct was that of an average officer under fire, excited but not unduly agitated or frightened." Not only were the officers not forthright or candid in their testimonies, according to the reporter, but they were also hypocritical: "I cannot refrain from remarking that the manner some of the officers have talked in private and to their friends in regard to the events of that day has been strangely at variance with their sworn testimony. It shows conclusively that they are either cowardly talking behind Reno's back, or else they have not courage enough to face his resentment by speaking the truth on the witness stand." In the end, he concluded, the major's attorney "claimed that the charges against Reno rested on the evidence of two mule packers, an Indian scout, a doctor, and an Indian interpreter. With the exception of the doctor, these were the sweepings of the army."[33]

After a long month of testimony, the court of inquiry ruled that there was insufficient evidence to "justify calling a court-martial to try Reno for cowardice and neglect of duty." It was beyond the court's ability to do so anyway, since the statute of limitations for a court martial had already expired. Any blundering on Reno's part was the "result of misapprehension not cowardice." Colonel John H. King, Ninth Infantry and president of the court, carefully concluded that while other officers of the Seventh Cavalry "had more brilliant displays of courage than Major Reno, there was nothing in his conduct which requires animadversion from this court."[34]

To achieve this unremarkable conclusion, Reno's defense had succeeded in bisecting the witnesses into two unequal camps—military and civilian. Either in support of the major or simply in order to recover the reputation of the regiment, the Seventh Cavalry's officers banded together and answered questions essentially in a single voice. These career military men cared less about rewriting the storyline of the infamous battle in order to protect Reno and more about defending the honor of the regiment, which, suspicion and gossip had it, had been brought low at the Little Big Horn by pride, jealousy, and divisiveness. This suited the purposes of the Division of the Missouri in Chicago (General Sheridan's office), which wanted to silence public discussion about the battle since it only served general antimilitary sentiments.[35] The cavalry officers had all but segregated themselves from the five civilian witnesses,

who chose not to withhold criticism of Reno in their individual testimonies. Any congeniality the officers shared with Porter en route
to Chicago was replaced during the courtroom proceedings with
poker faces and parsimonious testimony. Once regarded as a vital
member of the Seventh Cavalry solely responsible for the survival
of many of its wounded men, Porter found himself, in this moment
of judgment, standing outside a military wall of allegiance and an
exclusive fraternity.[36]

11

"Many Were Splendid Men"

WHEN MILITARY SURGEON AND HISTORIAN Colonel Percy M. Ashburn of the medical corps likened the army contract surgeon to the military mule, he meant no offense. On the contrary, he intended to illustrate his "poor and unsatisfactory" status:

> The mule, without pride of ancestry or hope of posterity, neither horse nor ass, unloved and unlovely, the recipient of contumelious language, was the Army's standby and salvation in the field in time of trouble.
>
> The contract surgeon's status was somewhat similar. Neither commissioned or enlisted, without regiment or corps, having no hope of promotion and dubious rank, they survived because they were needed, were respected for their personalities, were as necessary as the mules, harder worked, and quite as much an ever present help in trouble. They have never been accorded their just dues. Many were splendid men.[1]

The comparison was entirely apt, although its articulation was somewhat belated. Ashburn made these observations in his book *A History of the Medical Department of the United States Army,* published in 1929. By then, generations of underappreciated contract surgeons had served their country in the army during the Civil War, Indian Wars, Spanish-American War, and World War I. Ashburn's metaphor could only honor them in hindsight; it could not serve to help redress any of their grievances.

The tipping point for action actually had occurred forty-one years earlier. The Civil War was long over and the Indian campaigns in the West were winding down as the army forced the last of the tribes under firm reservation control. The number of contract surgeons had become sufficiently large for the men to be able to share experiences and grievances on a frequent basis and throughout the country. By 1888 they wove the common threads of their respective experiences into a uniform statement, which in turn inspired the formation of an official organization, the Association of Acting Assistant Surgeons of the United States Army. The time had come for the army's medical department to redress the injustices these surgeons had long suffered. The recorder for the association, W. Thornton Parker, phrased it bluntly: "these men deserved better treatment."[2]

The first annual meeting of the association took place in Newport, Rhode Island, home of the naval base and the stylish summer cottages of many of New York's elites. On the evening of June 24, 1889, members convened in the brown-shingled Casino centrally located on Bellevue Avenue. Professor A. Reeves Jackson, M.D., of Chicago presided over the meeting. Among the eleven surgeons who made up the newly formed council for the association was a North Dakotan, Henry Porter of Bismarck.

Porter had traveled far to attend the meeting of his colleagues and was undoubtedly proud to be a part of this protest against army maltreatment. Perhaps too he was delighted to spend time near an ocean. He was also a saddened man, whose plans for a happy domestic future had been dashed ten months earlier, in August 1888, when his wife, Charlotte, died of a heart-related illness. Porter now shared his stately home in Bismarck with his only child, seven-year-old Henry Viets Porter, commonly called Hallie. The recent widower had left private matters behind in order to attend the association meeting in Newport, where the main business was to hammer out a petition designed to bring about changes for current and future contract surgeons.

Always filling the chronic gaps in the army's medical corps, the "acting assistant surgeon has been a faithful and good worker," declared W. Thornton Parker, "with little to encourage him, except the reward of the consciousness of a duty faithfully performed, and of valuable services to the sick and the injured, rendered without adequate compensation." In the association's view, army contracts were arbitrarily assigned and annulled, most often at the demand of an army-weary Congress. Work was never steady for these physicians. Although in many ways comparable to second lieutenants, contract surgeons in fact enjoyed no formal rank, wore no uniform, had no retirement plan, and had no possibility of any kind of promotion. In a manner they became soldiers "in everything but . . . name and rank." Their families suffered too. Never legitimately eligible for proper quarters on the posts, the surgeon's wife and family had to be content with what was assigned to them, and even then be willing to vacate their quarters at any time should the most junior commissioned officer on the post request that housing.[3]

All of the association members in attendance had experienced slights, humiliations, and sheer indifference at the hands of the army. They felt they deserved better. Sitting side by side, elderly contract surgeons who had cared for soldiers during the Civil War as well as those who had ministered to soldiers policing the West identified three main areas of contention: pay and allowances, retirement, and commissions. Changes in these areas, they knew, would improve the status of contract surgeons. Such reforms would also "illustrate the wrongs they have endured."[4]

The Newport meeting produced a formal petition, which the authors intended "to lay before the military committee in congress at its next season." Section One addressed the issue of pay, requesting that contract surgeons receive the same pay allowed for a second lieutenant, mounted. Additionally, these physicians should be entitled forage for one horse and quarters "*permanently* assigned by the post commander during his service at the post."[5] Section Two took aim at the issue of retirement: after twenty years of service, contract surgeons should be eligible for "all the laws and regulations which apply to the retirement of surgeons and assistant surgeons of the army." Section Three spoke to the issue of army commissions, recommending that any contract surgeon currently in the service "may be appointed by the President and by and with the advice and consent of the Senate, an assistant surgeon . . . with the rank and pay of first lieutenant, mounted." Such a unique commission represented nothing short of a "reward for meritorious service." The petition to Congress, titled "An Act for the Relief of the Acting Assistant Surgeons in the Army," looked to secure proper recognition for the contract surgeon within the army's hierarchy and establish a level of security in the form of compensation: pay, retirement, and commission under certain conditions.

To garner publicity for its cause, the association published a slim volume entitled *Records,* edited by W. Thornton Parker, M.D. The book contained a copy of the formal petition to Congress along with letters of support from officers of the army such as Brigadier General Crook and General W. T. Sherman and an extract from a letter written by "Mrs. General Custer." All endorsed the requests made in the petition. Parker also compiled the biographies of many of the contract surgeons hired by the army. As intended by the association, these biographies answered "any imputation of inferiority in professional attainment" and helped substantiate a "deserving monument of honorable professional standing and faithful military service."[6] Colonel Ashburn's summation in his famous comparison of a mule and a contract surgeon—"Many were splendid men"—is attested to by these individual biographies.

Contract surgeons initially organized the association "with fond hope that even at this late date something of justice might be attained." Most interpreted "justice" to mean compensation. Some, however, also focused on a less quantifiable goal, one that reached into the obliquity of honor and posterity. For surgeons like Henry Porter, already eleven years past his final army contract and leading a highly successful civilian career, the organization appealed to him because of its stated goal to "secure a correct history of those who have served" with the army in the capacity of contract surgeons. And the "correct history" of the honorable records of these men merited formal and public recognition.[7]

Doctor Parker devoted part of his slim volume to an impassioned tribute to the contract surgeon: "He has shared the dangers of war, he has faced death on the battlefield, and has endured all the hardships of camp and garrison life."[8] These were the words of a former contract surgeon written to honor his colleagues as part of the "correct history." As such, they resonated with somber memories and recessed feelings still harbored by men like Porter.

At the Battle of the Little Big Horn, Porter had survived a race at breakneck speed through the timber and across the Little Big Horn River, only then to labor up the bluffs to the top of the hill. From the moment he dismounted his horse, he was entrusted with the medical care of every man on that hilltop. That was his sworn duty, and there was not another man on the scene who could have fulfilled it. Knowledge, skill, composure, and endurance were the essential strengths that he drew on intensively for more than twenty-one hours under appalling conditions during the combat on June 25 and 26, 1876. Demands on the lone surgeon never slackened during that time, and busy hands and an engaged mind may have helped keep at bay Porter's darker thoughts, those that lingered on how awfully tenuous it all was: the desperate efforts of the soldiers to protect themselves from nearly overwhelming rifle fire from below as well as from hilltops nearby, the vulnerable lives of so many wounded around him, and the seemingly long odds of survival. He was all too aware of several immediate agents of death: bullets, dehydration, and infection. What relief most of the cavalry experienced when the Indian village finally uprooted and migrated southward was for the surgeon only a short-lived feeling since he alone remained preoccupied with the ongoing survival of the men in his care.

Porter had ministered to his patients for inhumanly long hours even without the incentives of rank, promotion and commensurate pay, pension, and commission. He did his duty, it was noted in his short biography, "as faithfully and with the same professional efficacy as if [he] had been a regular commissioned officer."[9] To have the army formally honor the service of contract surgeons would have represented a form of justice in itself, and it might have sufficed to redress the slights and humiliations they had experienced. Like the mule, the contract surgeon was certainly the "Army's standby and salvation in the field in time of trouble," rarely idle, on the periphery, or out of touch with the soldiers. More often, surgical service was central and critical to any military undertaking.

He has "borne the burden and heat of the day."[10] That short phrase from the *Records* succinctly captures the experience of nearly every contract surgeon who had served with the army in the field. It is especially fitting for Henry Porter and his time of service with the Seventh Cavalry during the "Expedition against hostile Sioux" in the summer of 1876.

Epilogue

Holmes Offley Paulding, M.D., the only surgeon assigned to Colonel Gibbon's Montana column at the time of the Battle of the Little Big Horn, was serving at Fort Sidney, Nebraska, in April 1883 when he suffered an attack of acute rheumatism. On May 1, the physician attending Doctor Paulding noted that the patient had an "attack of syncope." At 5:00 P.M. on April 24, Paulding died very suddenly. Today the cause of death would be identified as acute myocardial infarction. Paulding was thirty-one years old. He is buried in St. Paul's Cemetery in Alexandria, Virginia.[1]

Captain Grant Marsh never again piloted the *Far West* after 1876. On October 20, 1883, the *Far West* hit a snag in the waters of the lower Missouri and sank. Marsh continued to pilot steamboats out of Bismarck until his death in 1916.[2]

Private Michael Madden, whose right leg Henry Porter amputated just below the knee, was discharged from the hospital at Fort Abraham Lincoln on September 13, 1876. He lived about seven more years, entering the U.S. Soldier's Home in Washington, DC, on August 15, 1877. He died at the age of forty-seven on December 18, 1883, and is buried in the Potter's Field section of the California, Missouri, cemetery.[3]

The horse **Comanche** recovered from his multiple wounds to become the pride of the Seventh Cavalry. Orders forbade anyone from riding him at any time. Comanche died on November 6, 1891, at the age of twenty-eight. His body was mounted and exhibited at the Chicago World's Fair in 1893. After that the horse assumed permanent residence at the University Museum, University of Kansas, Lawrence.[4]

Private Charles A. Windolph, Company H, became the longest-living survivor of the Battle of the Little Big Horn. He died on March 11, 1950, in Lead, South Dakota, at the age of ninety-nine.[5]

Doctor Henry R. Porter punctuated his successful medical career and business ventures in Bismarck with much travel. While visiting India during his second world tour, he fell ill in Calcutta and died on March 3, 1903, of heart-related illness in Agra, where he had hoped to see the Taj Mahal. He was buried there the following day. Although his son, Hal, wished to have his father's body embalmed and shipped to Oberlin, Ohio, to be buried next to his mother, the State Department advised that "while exhumation of the remains would be allowed, it was not advisable at this time."[6] To this day Henry Porter's remains lie in Agra.

In 1989, members of the Little Big Horn Associates—Dr. James Wengert, Elden Davis, and John M. Carroll—worked together to locate Porter's grave in the British Cantonment Cemetery in Agra. In cooperation with the State Department, the men arranged for a plaque to be erected at the gravesite. It reads:

> On 25–26 June 1876, Custer's 7th U.S. Cavalry suffered a defeat in battle with the Sioux, Cheyenne, and Arapahoe Indians, at the Battle of the Little Big Horn River, Montana, U.S.A. It is now famous in American folklore. As the only surviving medical

officer, Dr. Porter's surgical skill and cool personal bravery were responsible for preserving the lives of some 68 wounded men. He won the praise and respect of all surviving officers and men. We now add ours.[7]

Notes

Prologue

1. Donovan, *Terrible Glory,* 353. Material for the depiction of the court of inquiry is drawn from two sources, Nichols, *Reno Court of Inquiry,* and Davis and Davis, *Reno Court of Inquiry.*

2. Davis and Davis, *Reno Court of Inquiry,* 28.

3. J. S. Payne, captain in the Fifth Cavalry, was one of several men to testify who had not participated in the battle (along with Gibbon, Maguire, and Sheridan). He testified on the measurements of distances on the battlefield that he had taken in August 1878. Nichols, *Reno Court of Inquiry,* 272.

4. Taylor, *With Custer on the Little Bighorn,* 186.

Chapter 1

1. Barnett, *Touched by Fire,* 287. Unless otherwise noted, all numbers, statistics, and times of the day are taken from Gray, *Centennial Campaign.*

2. Carroll, *Custer's Chief of Scouts,* 62.

3. Donovan, *Terrible Glory,* 204; Carroll, *Custer's Chief of Scouts,* 64 (quote); Schoenberger, "Custer's Scouts," 41.

4. Horace Ellis, "A Survivor's Story of the Custer Massacre," *1876 Bighorn–Yellowstone Journal* 2 (Spring 1993): 7.

5. Wengert, "Contract Surgeon," 68; Hedren, "Sioux War Adventures of Dr. Charles V. Petteys," 30; Carson, *Furnishing Plan for the Post Surgeon's Quarters,* 56.

6. Hedren, *Great Sioux War Orders of Battle,* 92, 98.

7. "Interview with Henry Porter," *Minneapolis Tribune,* May 16, 1897, copy provided by Elden Davis.

8. Jerry L. Russell, *1876 Facts about Custer and the Battle of the Little Big Horn* (Mason City, Iowa: Savas, 1999), 76; Liddic, *Vanishing Victory,* 32.

9. Barnett, *Touched by Fire,* 301, 284; Liddic, *Vanishing Victory,* 8; Michno, *Encyclopedia of Indian Wars,* 295.

10. Gray, *Centennial Campaign,* 3.

Chapter 2

1. Wengert, "Contract Surgeon," 67, 68; Gillett, *Army Medical Department, 1818–1865,* 288; Parker, *Records of the Association of Acting Assistant Surgeons,* 37.

2. Wengert, "Contract Surgeon," 67–68. The oldest American surgical group, founded in 1880, is the American Surgical Association.

3. Ibid., 68; H. R. Porter to J. K. Barnes, July 6–Sept. 19, 1872, Henry R. Porter Papers, Entry 561, RG 94, National Archives and Records Administration (hereafter Porter Papers, NARA).

4. Gressley, "Soldier with Crook," 38 (first quote), 39 (second quote), 36 (fourth quote); Bourke, *On the Border with Crook,* 5 (third quote).

5. Bourke, *On the Border with Crook,* 180; Gressley, "Soldier with Crook," 40 (quote).

6. Schmitt, *General George Crook,* 174 (first quote), 176 (second quote).

7. Gressley, "Soldier with Crook," 41 (first quote). A copy of General Order No. 14 is found in Porter Papers, NARA.

8. Bourke, *On the Border with Crook,* 210 (quote); Gressley, "Soldier with Crook," 45.

9. Surgeon General's Office to H. R. Porter, Oct. 6, 1873, Porter Papers, NARA.

10. Langemo, *Bismarck,* 65.

11. Sherman and Thornson, *Plains Folk,* 335.

12. William J. Sloan to H. R. Porter, Sept. 28, 1875, Porter Papers, NARA; H. R. Porter, M.D., to Medical Director, Department of Dakota, Oct. 1, 1875, ibid.

Chapter 3

1. Andrist, *Long Death,* 241; Barnard, *Ten Years with Custer,* 169–70.

2. Merrill, *Spurs to Glory,* 196; Darling, *Custer's Seventh Cavalry Comes to Dakota,* 17 (quote), 19.

3. Barnard, *Ten Years with Custer,* 170; Darling, *Custer's Seventh Cavalry Comes to Dakota,* 199 (quote).

4. Arnold O. Goplen, *The Historical Significance of Fort Lincoln State Park* (Bismarck: North Dakota Parks and Recreation, 1946), 47–52.

5. Lubetkin, *Jay Cook's Gamble,* 283.

6. Utley, *Frontier Regulars,* 12.

7. Hammer, *Custer in '76,* 18–19.

8. Gray, *Centennial Campaign,* 25–27; Liddic, *Vanishing Victory,* 7.

9. Gray, *Centennial Campaign,* 29.

10. Hedren, *Great Sioux War Orders of Battle,* 34–40; Hutton, *Phil Sheridan & His Army,* 181 (quote).

Chapter 4

1. Luce, "Diaries and Letters of James M. DeWolf," 58.

2. H. R. Porter to Surgeon General, May 14, 1876, Porter Papers, NARA.

3. Gray, *Centennial Campaign,* 29.

4. Ibid., 74, 47, 110; Murray, *The Army Moves West,* 17; Hutchins, *Army and Navy Journal on the Battle of the Little Big Horn,* 24; Hedren, *Great Sioux War Orders of Battle,* 165.

5. Willert, *Little Big Horn Diary,* 3; Chorne, *Following the Custer Trail,* 14; Hedren, *Great Sioux War Orders of Battle,* 98.

6. Chorne, *Following the Custer Trail,* 10, 33, 84, 19.

7. Gray, "Medical Service of the Little Big Horn Campaign," 83.

8. Carson, *Furnishing Plan for the Post Surgeon's Quarters,* 54; Luce, "Diaries and Letters of James M. DeWolf," 34 (quote).

9. Ibid., 79, 81.

Chapter 5

1. The phrase in this chapter's title was used by Little Big Horn researcher Walter M. Camp in his "Address before the Annual Meeting and Dinner of the Order of Indian Wars, of the United States," which he delivered in Washington D.C. on January 17, 1920. Reprinted in Mary Ann Thompson, ed., *George Armstrong Custer's "Winners of the West" on the Battle of the Little Big Horn and Related Matters*, p. 83; Willert, *Little Big Horn Diary*, 264; Fox, *Archaeology, History, and Custer's Last Battle*, 297.

2. Gray, *Centennial Campaign*, 172.

3. The regimental standard was "furled and cased," carried safely by the pack train. See Hutchins, *Boots & Saddles at the Little Bighorn*, 59–62.

4. Nichols, *Reno Court of Inquiry*, 421.

5. Porter had purchased a "large Smith & Wesson pistol, the best made six shooter [that will] shoot accurate two hundred yards" in San Francisco in 1872 en route to Arizona Territory. See Gressley, "Soldier with Crook," 35. Porter must not have been carrying the revolver when he answered Reno.

6. Gray, *Centennial Campaign*, 173.

7. Michno, *Lakota Noon*, general reference map.

8. Hedren, *Great Sioux War Orders of Battle*, 78–79, 100–102.

9. Gray, *Centennial Campaign*, 141, 357.

10. Grace, *Army Surgeon's Manual*, 23; Walker, "Military Medicine at the Little Big Horn," 192.

11. Porter's surgical pocket case is preserved at the North Dakota State Historical Society in Bismarck. Several tools are missing from the case. Based on the known contents of similar pocket cases dating from the Civil War, I supplemented the names of the missing tools.

12. Brininstool, *Troopers with Custer*, 99; Hedren, *Great Sioux War Orders of Battle*, 28, 173.

13. Nichols, *Reno Court of Inquiry*, 190. John Gray identifies Porter's patient in the timber as "probably" Private George Lorentz, Company M. *Centennial Campaign*, 276. Lorentz was shot in the back of the neck, with the bullet exiting from his mouth. It is more likely that Porter tended to Private Henry Klotzbucher, Company M, as his wound was in the stom-

ach. See Brininstool, *Troopers with Custer,* 51; Liddic, *Vanishing Victory,* 76; and Nichols, *Men with Custer,* 182.

14. I have drawn the parallel between Major Reno's and Major Elliott's situations to try to reveal how Reno could have entertained the idea of abandonment. For fair and complete discussions of the Battle of Washita, see Greene, *Washita;* and Sandy Barnard, *A Hoosier Quaker Goes to War: The Life and Death of Major Joel H. Elliott, 7th Cavalry* (Wake Forest, N.C.: AST, 2010). Neither Greene nor Barnard draws any parallels between Reno and Elliott.

15. M. E. Terry, "A Brave Doctor," *Pioneer Press,* May 3, 1878, in *1876 Big Horn–Yellowstone Journal* 2 (Autumn 1993): 2.

16. Nichols, *Reno Court of Inquiry,* 30; Godfrey, "Custer's Last Battle," 371.

17. Nichols, *Reno Court of Inquiry,* 206, 191, 198.

18. Liddic, *Vanishing Victory,* 38.

19. Ibid., 122.

20. This interpretation of the battle is drawn from Donovan, *Terrible Glory.*

Chapter 6

1. Godfrey, "Custer's Last Battle," 377.

2. Barnard, *Ten Years with Custer,* 299.

3. Magnussen, *Peter Thompson's Narrative,* 203. The estimated size of the field hospital is based on archaeological finds of pack and saddle gear as well as nails from crates that may have been used to form some sort of protective perimeter. This information is courtesy of Douglas D. Scott. A standard basketball court is 50 × 94 feet, or 4,700 square feet. The space of the hilltop hospital was less than a quarter of a basketball court.

4. Brooks, *Civil War Medicine,* 65.

5. Rickey, *Forty Miles a Day,* 323; Porter to his parents, July 4, 1876, in *1876 Big Horn–Yellowstone Journal* 1 (Winter 1992): 3 (quote).

6. In 1877 Colonel Gibbon wrote about Reno's wounded: "Poor Fellows! An impression had, in some way, gained a footing amongst them during the long weary hours of the fight on the 26th that, to save the balance of

the command, they were to be abandoned." "Hunting Sitting Bull," 37. Edgar I. Stewart describes how Reno suggested the plan to Benteen in *Custer's Luck,* 420. In a letter to Godfrey dated January 3, 1886, Benteen suggests that Godfrey delete a detail from his forthcoming article for *Century Magazine:* "Don't you think that Reno has been sufficiently damned before the country that it can well be afforded to leave out in the article the proposition from him to saddle up and leave the field of the Little Big Horn on the 1st night of the fight?" Windolph, *I Fought with Custer,* 203. Godfrey spells out the awful secret: " Reno came to [Benteen] and proposed to march away on the back trail . . . mount all the men who could ride, and *abandon the wounded* who were unable to ride or would delay the march of the retreat." Ibid., 205.

7. Carroll, *Sunshine Magazine Articles,* 13.

8. Having been badly wounded in the Battle of the Rosebud on June 17, an immobilized Captain Guy V. Henry recalled the horror of overhearing preparations for the burial of dead soldiers. See Henry, "Adventures of Army and Navy Officers: Wounded in an Indian Fight," in *Big Horn–Yellowstone Journal* 3 (Winter 1994): 3.

9. La Garde, *Gunshot Injuries,* 100; Olch, "Medicine in the Indian-Fighting Army," 38; Return of Wounds and Injuries Received in Action, Battle of the Little Big Horn, Entry 13, Surgeon General of the Army, RG 94, NARA; Williams, *Military Register of Custer's Last Command,* 251.

10. La Garde, *Gunshot Injuries,* 55; Reedstrom, *Bugles, Banners, & Warbonnets,* 193 (quote). La Garde was a Great Sioux War veteran like Porter and was later commissioned.

11. Bollet, *Civil War Medicine,* 200.

12. Rothstein, *American Physicians in the Nineteenth Century,* 252.

13. "Story of the Big Horn Campaign of 1876: As Told by Private Daniel Newell, of Company M, 7th U.S. Cavalry, To John P. Everett," in Carroll, *Sunshine Magazine Articles,* 13; Taylor, *With Custer on the Little Bighorn,* 59; Sklenar, *To Hell with Honor,* 57.

14. Hammer, *Custer in '76,* 225.

15. Return of Wounds and Injuries Received in Action, Battle of the Little Big Horn, NARA.

16. Olch, "Medicine in the Indian-Fighting Army," 38–39.

17. Bollet, *Civil War Medicine,* 198; Smith, *Handbook of Surgical Operations,* 260.

18. Windolph, *I Fought with Custer,* 106.

19. "Henry R. Porter," *Compendium of History and Biography of North Dakota,* 163.

20. Windolph, *I Fought with Custer,* 107 (quote); Mulford, *Fighting Indians in the 7th United States Cavalry,* 19; Robertson, *Tenting Tonight,* 86.

21. Karen L. Davis and E. Elden Davis, "The Battle on the Little Big Horn," *1876 Big Horn–Yellowstone Journal* 1 (Winter 1992): 4 (first quote); "A Surgeon Tells of a Day and Night with Reno," *St. Paul Pioneer Press,* Aug. 16, 1891 (second quote), copy provided by Elden Davis.

Chapter 7

1. Windolph, *I Fought with Custer,* 77 (first quote); Thompson, *Custer's "Winners of the West,"* 192 (second quote).

2. Barnard, *Ten Years with Custer,* 300.

3. Schoenberger, "A Trooper with Custer," 70.

4. Godfrey, "Custer's Last Battle," 382.

5. Sigerist, "Surgery at the Time of the Introduction of Antisepsis," 173.

6. Godfrey, "Custer's Last Battle," 382.

7. Gillett, "United States Army Surgeons and the Big Horn–Yellowstone Expedition," 20.

8. Buecker, "Surgeon at the Little Big Horn," 36 (first quote), 39 (second quote); Boyes, *Surgeon's Diary,* 14 (third quote).

9. Buecker, "Surgeon at the Little Big Horn," 38.

10. Smith, *Handbook of Surgical Operations,* 99.

11. Stemen, *Railroad Surgery,* 163.

12. Gray, *Centennial Campaign,* 279; Return of Wounds and Injuries Received in Action, Battle of the Little Big Horn, NARA; Hammer, *Custer in '76,* 236; Walker, "Military Medicine at the Little Bighorn," 192.

13. Smith, *Handbook of Surgical Operations,* 99. Douglas D. Scott discovered that Porter performed the flap method using lateral flaps when

he examined Madden's discharge notice. See "'An Agreeable Sort When Sober,'" 32.

14. Marquis, *Two Days after the Custer Battle*, 4; Brieger, "American Surgery and the Germ Theory of Disease," 145 (quote).

15. Return of Wounds and Injuries Received in Action, Battle of the Little Big Horn, NARA.

16. Carroll, *Sunshine Magazine Articles*, 15.

17. Gray, "Captain Clifford's Story—Part II," 82.

18. Reedstrom, *Bugles, Banners, & Warbonnets*, 214.

19. Guy V. Henry, "Adventures of American Army and Navy Officers: Wounded in an Indian Fight," *Big Horn–Yellowstone Journal* 3 (Winter 1994): 3, 5.

20. Gillett, *Army Medical Department, 1865–1917*, 71.

21. Michno, "Space Warp," 25, 28; Scott, Willey, and Connor, *They Died with Custer*, 38.

22. Hammer, *Custer in '76*, 140; Scott, Willey, and Connor, *They Died with Custer*, 25.

23. Kramer, "Germ Theory and the Early Public Health Program," 233.

24. Clendening, *Source Book of Medical History*, 612; Rothstein, *American Physicians in the Nineteenth Century*, 263.

25. Kramer, "Germ Theory and the Early Public Health Program," 234.

26. Dr. Semmelweis revealed this awful truth in 1847 in his study of puerperal fever. See Nuland, *Doctor's Plague*.

27. Willert, *March of the Columns*, 30.

28. Gibbon, "Hunting Sitting Bull," 36.

29. Gray, "Captain Clifford's Story—Part II," 83.

30. Rickey, *Forty Miles a Day*, 328.

31. Otis, *Report to the Surgeon General on the Transport of the Sick and Wounded by Pack Animals*, 22; Gillett, "United States Army Surgeons and the Big Horn–Yellowstone Expedition," 20.

32. Magnussen, *Peter Thompson's Narrative*, 273.

33. Gibbon, "Hunting Sitting Bull," 44.

34. Willert, *March of the Columns*, 40.

35. Gray, "Captain Clifford's Story—Part II," 83.

36. Hanson, *Conquest of the Missouri*, 295–96.

Chapter 8

1. Hanson, *Conquest of the Missouri*, 298. Terry's number is inaccurate, off by ten men. Most likely he was unaware of the soldiers who had been released by the medical service and had rejoined their companies.

2. Scott, Willey, and Connor, *They Died with Custer*, 12.

3. Hanson, *Conquest of the Missouri*, 133, 238, 244; "Murray, *The Army Moves West*, 6 (quote). In 1858–59 Marsh worked with "Sam" Clemens as his second pilot onboard the *A. B. Chambers No. 2*. Hanson, *Conquest of the Missouri*, 27.

4. "Interview with Grant Marsh," *Bismarck Tribune*, Mar. 21, 1898 (quote), copy provided by Elden Davis; Hanson, *Conquest of the Missouri*, 238.

5. Willert, *March of the Columns*, 43.

6. Hanson, *Conquest of the Missouri*, 115, 239.

7. Hedren, *Great Sioux War Orders of Battle*, 92; Hanson, *Conquest of the Missouri*, 102 (quote), 304; Lass, "Steamboats on the Yellowstone," 38. There was a minor change among Porter's forty-two patients: the Crow scout White Swan was left ashore, but the consumptive Sergeant Rigney, 7th Infantry, took his place. Gray, *Centennial Campaign*, 282.

8. Carroll, *Sunshine Magazine Articles*, 27; Willert, *March of the Columns*, 58.

9. Carroll, *Sunshine Magazine Articles*, 15; *The Soldier's Handbook*, quoted in Rickey, *Forty Miles a Day*, 325.

10. Hedren, *Great Sioux War Orders of Battle*, 92–93.

11. Carroll, *Sunshine Magazine Articles*, 27 (quote); Gray, *Centennial Campaign*, 282.

12. Hanson, *Conquest of the Missouri*, 306.

13. "Reminiscences of the Custer Massacre," *Bismarck Tribune*, Mar. 21, 1898, copy provided by Elden Davis.

14. Hanson, *Conquest of the Missouri*, 306; Gray, *Centennial Campaign*, 283; "Interview with Grant Marsh," *Bismarck Tribune*, Mar. 21, 1898 (quote), copy provided by Elden Davis; Fort Abraham Lincoln Post Returns, July 1876, Roll 628, Microcopy 617, NARA.

15. "Flashed News of CUSTER MASSACRE First to World," in *Big Horn–Yellowstone Journal* 2 (Summer 1993): 21.

16. Lane, "Custer's Massacre," 46; Knight, *Following the Indian Wars,* 194–95; Hanson, *Conquest of the Missouri,* 308 (quote).

17. Walker, *Dr. Henry R. Porter,* 58 (quote); "Flashed News of CUSTER MASSACRE First to World," 21; Hanson, *Conquest of the Missouri,* 308; Knightly, *First Casualty,* 23.

18. Scott et al., *Archaeological Perspectives on the Battle of the Little Big Horn,* 23.

19. Ashburn, *History of the Medical Department,* 132; Carson, *Furnishing Plan for the Post Surgeon's Quarters,* 43 (first quote); McMahon and Rutecki, "In Anticipation of the Germ Theory," 5 (second quote).

20. Chambers, *Fort Abraham Lincoln,* 102.

21. Donovan, *Terrible Glory,* 470.

22. Carroll, *Sunshine Magazine Articles,* 27. Louise Barnett identifies the twenty-four widows at the fort. See *Touched by Fire,* 306–307.

23. Hanson, *Conquest of the Missouri,* 314.

24. Walker, *Dr. Henry R. Porter,* 63.

Chapter 9

1. Porter's letters to Fanny DeWolf are found in the DeWolf Collection, White Swan Library, Little Bighorn Battlefield National Monument.

2. Ibid.

3. Murray, *The Army Moves West,* 7.

4. Michno, "Space Warp," 23, 25, 28.

5. Willert, *March of the Columns,* 427. Weir died on December 9, 1876, at age thirty-eight.

6. Gillett, "United States Army Surgeons and the Big Horn–Yellowstone Expedition," 22; Willert, *March of the Columns,* 154; Utley, *Frontier Regulars,* 198.

7. Tate, *Frontier Army in the Settlement of the West,* 179. The camp's doctors are identified in Hedren, *Great Sioux War Orders of Battle,* 120–22.

8. Willert, *March of the Columns,* 308.

9. Ibid., 239.

10. Ibid., 268.

11. Ibid., 300.

12. Ibid., xi; Hedren, *Great Sioux War Orders of Battle,* 117–23.

13. Willert, *March of the Columns,* 306.

14. Barnett, *Touched by Fire,* 303; Willert, *March,* 305.

15. Willert, *March of the Columns,* 337.

16. Ibid., 336.

17. Ibid., 337.

18. Greene, *Slim Buttes,* 3; Hedren, *Great Sioux War Orders of Battle,* 100–104.

19. Willert, *March of the Columns,* 345.

20. Ibid., xi.

21. Ibid., 340.

22. Ibid., 349 (quote), 358, 374, 364.

23. Finerty, *Warpath and Bivouac,* 266.

24. Willert, *March of the Columns,* 379.

25. Scott, Willey, Connor, *They Died with Custer,* 63, 278 (first quote), 277 (second quote); Hedren, *Great Sioux War Orders of Battle,* 33.

26. Freemon, *Gangrene and Glory,* 231.

27. Willert, *March of the Columns,* 412.

28. Ibid., 398 (first quote), 400 (Wasson quotes).

29. Ibid., 425.

30. Ibid., 432–33 (first quote), 434 (second and third quotes), 435 (fourth quote).

31. Ibid., 438–39.

32. Boyes, *Surgeon's Diary,* 29.

33. It is my conjecture that Porter separated from the Seventh Cavalry at this point to accompany the sick men back to Fort Abraham Lincoln. It fits with the fact that he answered a letter to Fanny DeWolf on September 14, having likely picked up his mail at the fort around September 12. On September 26—two weeks later—the Seventh Cavalry arrived back at the fort.

34. Brooks, *Civil War Medicine,* 127; Bollet, *Civil War Medicine,* 240.

35. Gillett, *Army Medical Department, 1865–1917,* 74.

36. Ibid., 40.

Chapter 10

1. William J. Sloan to Surgeon General, Sept. 30, 1876, Porter Papers, NARA; Gillett, *Army Medical Department, 1865–1917,* 16.

2. Gillett, *Army Medical Department, 1865–1917,* 16.

3. Contract between Chief Medical Officer, Expedition against hostile Sioux, and Dr. H. R. Porter, May 15, 1876, Porter Papers, NARA.

4. "Military History of Dr. Henry R. Porter, Late A.A. Surgeon, U.S.A., as Shown by the Records of the Office," July 19, 1880, Porter Papers, NARA.

5. Saum, "Private John F. Donohue's Reflections," 51.

6. Graham, *Custer Myth,* 181 (first quote); "Henry R. Porter," 164 (second quote).

7. Robinson, *History of North Dakota,* 183, 127, 132.

8. Walker, *Dr. Henry R. Porter,* 30.

9. H. R. Porter to Mrs. Fanny J. DeWolf, Sept. 12, 1876, DeWolf Collection, White Swan Library, Little Bighorn Battlefield National Monument.

10. Scott, "'An Agreeable Sort When Sober,'" 32.

11. Walker, *Dr. Henry R. Porter,* 63.

12. Sloan's correspondences are found in Porter Papers, NARA. On November 18, 1876, Sloan wrote to Surgeon General Barnes about the battles and expeditions in the fall that had strained his medical department. See Bailey, *Pacifying the Plains,* 167.

13. William J. Sloan to H. R. Porter, Nov. 18, 1876, Porter Papers, NARA.

14. Gillett, *Army Medical Department, 1865–1917,* 16.

15. William J. Sloan to Surgeon General, Feb. 28, 1877, Porter Papers, NARA.

16. Walker, *Dr. Henry R. Porter,* 9.

17. Kimball and Gorgas, *Soldier-Doctor of Our Army,* 29.

18. Gillett, *Army Medical Department 1869–1917,* 13; Carson, *Furnishing Plan for the Post Surgeon's Quarters,* 56; Hedren, "Sioux War Adventures of Dr. Charles V. Petteys," 35.

19. Walker, *Dr. Henry R. Porter,* 5, 6.

20. H. R. Porter to Surgeon General, Jan. 8, 1878, Porter Papers, NARA (quote); "Henry R. Porter," 164; Moffett, "Henry R. Porter," 9; "Doctor

Porter in Luck," *Bismarck Daily Tribune,* June 1, 1889, copy provided by Elden Davis.

21. Utley, *Custer and the Great Controversy,* 41 (first quote); Downey, *Indian-Fighting Army,* 34 (second quote); Olch, "Medicine in the Indian-Fighting Army," 33.

22. Gibbon, "Hunting Sitting Bull," 61.

23. *Little Big Horn–Yellowstone Journal* 2 (Spring 1993): 14.

24. Willert, *March of the Columns,* 379 (first quote), 374, 424 (second quote).

25. Ibid., 590–92.

26. Davis and Davis, *Reno Court of Inquiry,* 13.

27. "The Custer Massacre," *Chicago Times,* Jan. 13, 1879 (first and second quotes), copy provided by Elden Davis; Andrist, *Long Death,* 283; "Opinions Differ," *St. Paul Globe,* Jan. 13, 1879 (third quote), copy provided by Elden Davis.

28. Davis and Davis, *Reno Court of Inquiry,* 37.

29. Ibid., 62.

30. "New York Mills Correspondence," *Rome (N.Y.) Citizen,* Feb. 7, 1879, copy provided by Elden Davis.

31. Davis and Davis, *Reno Court of Inquiry,* 63 (first quote); Nichols, *Reno Court of Inquiry,* 191 (second quote).

32. Davis and Davis, *Reno Court of Inquiry,* 63–65.

33. Ibid., 71–72, 84, 98.

34. Ibid., 97, 98, 101.

35. Barnett, *Touched by Fire,* 311.

36. Adams, *Class and Race in the Frontier Army,* 21.

Chapter 11

1. Ashburn, *History of the Medical Department,* 150–51.

2. Parker, *Records of the Association of Acting Assistant Surgeons,* v.

3. Ibid., 5 (first quote); Ames, "Acting Assistant Surgeon of the Army of the United States," 121 (second quote); Wier, "Nineteenth Century Army Doctors on the Frontier and in Nebraska," 211.

4. Parker, *Records of the Association of Acting Assistant Surgeons,* vi.

5. Ibid., 149.

6. Ibid., v.

7. Ibid., vi, 6.

8. Ibid., 5.

9. Ibid., 6.

10. Ibid.

Epilogue

1. Boyes, *Surgeon's Diary,* 32–33.

2. Hanson, *Conquest of the Missouri,* 366.

3. Nichols, *Men with Custer,* 202; Wilson, "Marker Dedicated at Grave of Little Bighorn Survivor," 8.

4. Hatch, *Custer and the Battle of the Little Bighorn,* 31.

5. Nichols, *Men with Custer,* 361.

6. *Bismarck Daily Tribune,* Mar. 9, 1903, copy provided by Elden Davis.

7. *Little Big Horn Associates Newsletter,* vol. 23, Aug. 1989, 8, copy provided by Elden Davis.

Bibliography

Archives

National Archives and Records Administration, Washington, D.C.
Fort Abraham Lincoln Post Returns, July 1876. Roll 628. Microcopy 617.
Henry R. Porter Papers. Entry 561. Surgeon General of the Army, RG 94.
Return of Wounds and Injuries Received in Action, Battle of Little Big Horn. Entry 13. Surgeon General of the Army, RG 94.
White Swan Library, Little Bighorn Battlefield National Monument, Crow Agency, Mont. DeWolf Collection.

Books

Adams, Kevin. *Class and Race in the Frontier Army: Military Life in the West, 1870–1890.* Norman: University of Oklahoma Press, 2009.
Agnew, Jeremy. *Life of a Soldier on the Western Frontier.* Missoula, Mont.: Mountain, 2008.
Andrist, Ralph K. *The Long Death: The Last Days of the Plains Indians.* Norman: University of Oklahoma Press, 2001.
Ashburn, Percy M. *A History of the Medical Department of the United States Army.* Boston: Houghton Mifflin, 1929.
Bailey, John W. *Pacifying the Plains: General Alfred Terry and the Decline of the Sioux, 1866–1890.* Westport, Conn.: Greenwood, 1979.

Barnard, Sandy, ed. *Ten Years with Custer: A 7th Cavalryman's Memoirs.* Terre Haute, Ind.: AST, 2001.

Barnett, Louise. *Touched by Fire: The Life, Death, and Mythic Afterlife of George Armstrong Custer.* New York: Henry Holt, 1996.

Bayne-Jones, Stanhope, M.D. *The Evolution of Preventive Medicine in the United States Army, 1607–1939.* Washington, D.C.: Office of the Surgeon General, Department of the Army, 1968.

Billings, John Shaw. *A Report on Barracks and Hospitals with Descriptions of Military Posts.* Washington, D.C.: Government Printing Office, 1870.

Bollet, Alfred Jay, M.D. *Civil War Medicine: Challenges and Triumphs.* Tucson: Galen, 2002.

Bonner, Thomas Neville. *The Kansas Doctor. A Century of Pioneering.* Lawrence: University Press of Kansas, 1959.

Bourke, John G. *On the Border with Crook.* New York: Charles Scribners & Sons, 1892.

Boyes, W. ed. *Surgeon's Diary with the Custer Relief Column.* Washington, D.C.: South Capital, 1974.

Brandes, Ray. *Frontier Military Posts of Arizona.* Dale Stuart King, 1960.

Brininstool, E. A. *Troopers with Custer: Historic Incidents of the Battle of the Little Big Horn.* 1952. Reprint, Mechanicsburg, Pa.: Stackpole, 1994.

Brooks, Stewart. *Civil War Medicine.* Springfield: Charles C. Thomas, 1966.

Bulloch, William, M.D., F.R.S. *The History of Bacteriology.* New York: Dover, 1979.

Byrne, Bernard James, M.D. *A Frontier Army Surgeon.* New York: Exposition, 1935.

Carroll, John M. *Custer in Periodicals: A Bibliographic Checklist.* Fort Collins, Colo.: Old Army Press, 1975.

———, ed. *Custer's Chief of Scouts.* Lincoln: University of Nebraska Press, 1982.

———, ed. *The Sunshine Magazine Articles.* Bryan, Tex.: Privately Printed.

Carson, Nan V. *Furnishing Plan for the Post Surgeon's Quarters: Fort Laramie National Historic Site.* Omaha: Midwest Regional Office, National Park Service, 1963.

Cassedy, James H. *Medicine in America: A Short History.* Baltimore: The John Hopkins University Press, 1991.

Chambers, Lee. *Fort Abraham Lincoln: Dakota Territory.* Atglen, Pa.: Schiffer, 2008.

Chandler, Melbourne C. *Of Garry Owen in Glory: The History of the 7th U.S. Cavalry.* Annandale, Va.: Turnpike, 1960.

Chorne, Laudie J. *Following the Custer Trail of 1876.* Bismarck, N.Dak.: Trails West, 2001.

Clarke, Edward H. *A Century of Medicine, 1776–1876.* Philadelphia: Henry C. Lea, 1876.

Clendening, Logan, M.D. *Source Book of Medical History.* New York: Paul H. Hoeber, 1942.

Coffman, Edward M. *The Old Army: A Portrait of the American Army in Peacetime, 1784–1898.* New York: Oxford University Press, 1986.

Connell, Evan S. *Son of the Morning Star.* San Francisco: North Point, 1984.

Cozzens, Peter, ed. *Eyewitness to the Indian Wars, 1865–1890: The Long War for the Northern Plains.* Harrisburg, Pa.: Stackpole, 2004.

Darling, Roger. *Custer's Seventh Cavalry Comes to Dakota.* El Segundo, Calif.: Upton and Sons, 1989.

Davis, Karen L., and E. Elden Davis, eds. *The Reno Court of Inquiry: The Pioneer Press, St. Paul and Minneapolis, 1878–1879.* Howell, Mich.: Powder River, 1993.

Donovan, James. *A Terrible Glory.* New York: Little, Brown, 2008.

Downey, Fairfax. *Indian-Fighting Army.* Fort Collins, Colo.: Old Army Press, 1971.

Duffin, Jacalyn. *Langstaff: A Nineteenth Century Medical Life.* Toronto: University of Toronto Press, 1993.

Dunlop, Richard. *Doctors of the American Frontier.* New York: Doubleday, 1965.

Farmer, Laurence, M.D. *Master Surgeon: A Biography of Joseph Lister.* New York: Harper & Brothers, 1962.

Faust, Drew Gilpin. *This Republic of Suffering.* New York: Alfred A. Knopf, 2008.

Finerty, John F. *Warpath and Bivouac.* Edited by Milo Milton Quaife. Lincoln: University of Nebraska Press, 1966.

Fougera, Katherine Gibson. *With Custer's Cavalry.* Lincoln: University of Nebraska Press, 1986.

Fox, Richard Allan, Jr. *Archaeology, History, and Custer's Last Battle.* Norman: University of Oklahoma Press, 1993.

Frazer, Robert W. *Forts of the West.* Norman: University of Oklahoma Press, 1965.

Freemon, Frank R. *Gangrene and Glory: Medical Care during the American Civil War.* Madison, N.J.: Fairleigh Dickinson University Press, 1998.

Frost, Lawrence A. *The Custer Album: A Pictorial Biography of General George A. Custer.* New York: Bonanza, 1984.

Gillett, Mary C. *The Army Medical Department, 1818–1865.* Washington, D.C.: Center of Military History, US Army, 1987.

———. *The Army Medical Department, 1865–1917.* Washington, D.C.: Center of Military History, US Army, 1995.

Grace, William. *The Army Surgeon's Manual.* New York: Baillière Brothers, 1864.

Graham, W. A. *The Custer Myth: A Source Book of Custeriana.* New York: Bonanza, 1953.

Gray, John S. *Centennial Campaign: The Sioux War of 1876.* Fort Collins, Colo.: Old Army Press, 1976.

Greene, Jerome A., ed. *Indian War Veterans: Memories of Army Life and Campaigns in the West, 1864–1898.* New York: Savas Beatie, 2007.

———. *Slim Buttes, 1876: An Episode of the Great Sioux War.* Norman: University of Oklahoma Press, 1982.

———. *Washita: The U.S. Army and the Southern Cheyennes, 1867–1879.* Norman: University of Oklahoma Press, 2004.

Hammer, Kenneth, ed. *Custer in '76: Walter Camp's Notes on the Custer Fight.* Salt Lake City: Brigham Young University Press, 1976.

———. *The Springfield Carbine of the Western Frontier.* Fort Collins, Colo.: Old Army Press, 1970.

Hanson, Joseph Mills. *The Conquest of the Missouri.* Chicago: A. C. McClurg, 1910.

Hardorff, Richard G., ed. *Walter M. Camp's Little Bighorn Rosters.* Spokane: Arthur H. Clark, 2002.

Hatch, Thom. *Custer and the Battle of the Little Bighorn.* Jefferson, N.C.: McFarland, 2000.

Hedren, Paul L., ed. *The Great Sioux War: The Best from "Montana The Magazine of Western History."* Helena: Montana Historical Society Press, 1991.

———. *Great Sioux War Orders of Battle: How the United States Army Waged War on the Northern Plains, 1876–1877.* Norman, Okla.: Arthur H. Clark, 2011.

———. *We Trailed the Sioux: Enlisted Men Speak on Custer, Crook, and the Great Sioux War.* Mechanicsburg, Pa.: Stackpole, 2003.

Hutchins, James S., ed. *The Army and Navy Journal on the Battle of the Little Big Horn and Related Matters, 1876–1881.* El Segundo, Calif.: Upton and Sons, 2003.

———. *Boots & Saddles at the Little Bighorn.* Fort. Collins, Colo.: Old Army Press, 1976.

Hutton, Paul Andrew. *Phil Sheridan & His Army.* Norman: University of Oklahoma Press, 1985.

———, ed. *Soldiers West. Biographies from the Military Frontier.* Lincoln: University of Nebraska Press, 1987.

Jacobson, Walter Hamilton Acland. *The Operations of Surgery: A Systematic Handbook for Practitioners, Students, & Hospital Surgeons.* Philadelphia: P. Blakiston and Son, 1889.

Kain, Robert C. *In the Valley of the Little Big Horn: The 7th and the Sioux, June 25–26, 1876.* North Hollywood, Calif.: Beinfeld, 1978.

Karolevitz, Robert F. *Doctors of the Old West.* Seattle: Superior, 1967.

Kershaw, Robert J. *Red Sabbath: The Battle of the Little Big Horn.* Hersham, Surrey: Ian Allen, 2005.

Kimball, Maria Brace, and William C. Gorgas. *A Soldier-Doctor of Our Army: James P. Kimball, Late Colonel and Assistant Surgeon-General, U.S. Army.* Boston: Houghton-Mifflin, 1917.

King, Lester S. *American Medicine Comes of Age, 1840–1920.* [Chicago]: American Medical Association, 1984.

———. *Transformations in American Medicine from Benjamin Rush to William Osler.* Baltimore: The Johns Hopkins University Press, 1991.

Knight, Oliver. *Following the Indian Wars.* Norman: University of Oklahoma Press, 1960.

Knightly, Phillip. *The First Casualty: The War Correspondent as Hero and Myth-Maker from the Crimea to Kosovo.* Baltimore: The Johns Hopkins University Press, 2002.

Koury, Michael J. *Diaries of the Little Big Horn.* Bellevue, Neb.: Old Army Press, 1969.

La Garde, Louis A. *Gunshot Injuries: How They Are Inflicted, Their Complications and Treatment.* New York: William Wood, 1916.

Langemo, Cathy A. *Bismarck, North Dakota: Images of America.* Chicago: Arcadia, 2002.

Liddic, Bruce R. *Vanishing Victory: Custer's Final March.* El Segundo, Calif.: Upton and Sons, 2004.

Lubetkin, M. John. *Jay Cooke's Gamble: The Northern Pacific Railroad, the Sioux, and the Panic of 1873.* Norman: University of Oklahoma Press, 2006.

Magnussen, Daniel O., ed. *Peter Thompson's Narrative of the Little Bighorn Campaign of 1876.* Glendale, Calif.: Arthur H. Clark, 1974.

Marquis, Thomas B. *Custer on the Little Bighorn.* Lodi, Calif.: J. L. Hastings, 1967.

———. *Two Days after the Custer Battle.* Scottsdale, Ariz.: Cactus Pony, 1933.

Merrill, James M. *Spurs to Glory: The Story of the United States Cavalry.* Chicago: Rand McNally, 1966.

Michno, Gregory F. *Encyclopedia of Indian Wars: Western Battles and Skirmishes, 1850–1890.* Missoula, Mont.: Mountain, 2003.

———. *Lakota Noon: The Indian Narrative of Custer's Defeat.* Missoula, Mont.: Mountain, 1997.

Mulford, A. F. *Fighting Indians in the 7th United States Cavalry.* Corning, N.Y.: Paul Lindsley Mulford, 1879.

Murray, Robert A. *The Army Moves West: Supplying the Western Indian Wars Camapigns.* Fort Collins, Colo.: Old Army Press, 1981.

Nichols, Ronald H., ed. *Men with Custer.* Hardin, Mont.: Custer Battlefield Historical and Museum Association, 2000.

———, comp. and ed. *Reno Court of Inquiry.* Hardin, Mont.: Custer Battlefield Historical and Museum Association, 1996.

Nuland, Sherwin B. *The Doctor's Plague: Germs, Childbed Fever, and the Strange Story of Ignac Semmelweis*. New York: W. W. Norton, 2003.

Nye, Elwood L. *Marching with Custer: A Day-by-Day Evaluation of the Uses, Abuses, and Conditions of the Animals on the Ill-fated Expedition of 1876*. Glendale, Calif.: Arthur H. Clarke, 1964.

Otis, George A. *A Report of Surgical Cases Treated in the United States Army from 1865 to 1871*. Washington, D.C.: Government Printing Office, 1871.

———. *A Report to the Surgeon General on the Transport of Sick and Wounded by Pack Animals*. Washington, D.C.: Government Printing Office, 1877.

Parker, W. Thornton, M.D., ed. *Records of the Association of Acting Assistant Surgeons of the United States Army*. Salem, Mass., 1891.

Pusey, William Allen. *A Doctor of the 70s and 80s*. Springfield, Ill.: Charles C. Thomas, 1932.

Quebbeman, Francis E. *Medicine in Territorial Arizona*. Phoenix: Arizona Historical Foundation, 1966.

Reedstrom, Ernest Lisle. *Bugles, Banners, & Warbonnets*. New York: Bonanza, 1986.

Reilly, Hugh J. *The Frontier Newspapers and the Coverage of the Plains Indian Wars*. Santa Barbara, Calif.: Praeger, 2010.

Rickey, Don, Jr. *Forty Miles a Day on Beans and Hay*. Norman: University of Oklahoma Press, 1963.

Robertson, James I., Jr. *Tenting Tonight: The Soldier's Life*. Alexandria, Va.: Time-Life Books, 1984.

Robinson, Elwyn B. *History of North Dakota*. Lincoln: University of Nebraska Press, 1966.

Rothstein, William G. *American Physicians in the Nineteenth Century: From Sects to Science*. Baltimore: The Johns Hopkins University Press, 1972.

Schmitt, Martin F., ed. *General George Crook: His Autobiography*. Norman: University of Oklahoma Press, 1946.

Scott, Douglas D., Richard A. Fox Jr., Melissa A. Connor, and Dick Harmon. *Archaeological Perspectives on the Battle of the Little Bighorn*. Norman: University of Oklahoma Press, 1989.

Scott, Douglas D., P. Willey; and Melissa A. Connor. *They Died with Custer.* Norman: University of Oklahoma Press, 1998.

Sherman, William C., and Playford V. Thorson, eds. *Plains Folk: North Dakota's Ethnic History.* Fargo: North Dakota State University, 1988.

Sklenar, Larry. *To Hell with Honor: Custer and the Little Bighorn.* Norman: University of Oklahoma Press, 2000.

Smith, Stephen, M.D. *Handbook of Surgical Operations.* New York: Baillière Brothers, 1863.

Sohn, Anton Paul. *A Saw, Pocket Instruments, and Two Ounces of Whiskey: Frontier Military Medicine in the Great Basin.* Spokane: Arthur H. Clarke, 1998.

Starr, Paul. *The Social Transformation of American Medicine.* New York: Basic Books, 1982.

Stemen, Christian Berry. *Railway Surgery; a Practical Work on the Special Department of Railway Surgery: for Railway Surgeons and Practitioners in the General Practice of Surgery.* St. Louis: J. H. Chambers, 1890.

Stewart, Edgar I. *Custer's Luck.* Norman: University of Oklahoma Press, 1955.

Stewart, Miller J. *Moving the Wounded: Litters, Cacolets, & Ambulance Wagons, U.S. Army, 1776–1876.* Fort Collins, Colo.: Old Army Press, 1979.

Tate, Michael. *The Frontier Army in the Settlement of the West.* Norman: University of Oklahoma Press, 1999.

Taylor, William O. *With Custer on the Little Bighorn.* New York: Penguin, 1996.

Terry, Alfred H. *Field Diary of General Alfred H. Terry: The Yellowstone Expedition—1876.* Bellevue, Neb.: Old Army Press, 1970.

Thompson, Mary Ann, ed. *George Armstrong Custer's "Winners of the West" on the Battle of the Little Big Horn and Related Matters.* El Segundo, Calif.: Upton and Sons, 2007.

Tripler, Charles S., and George C. Blackman. *Handbook for the Military Surgeon.* Cincinnati: Robert Clarke, 1862.

Upton, Richard, ed. *The Battle of the Little Big Horn & Custer's Last Fight Remembered by Participants at the Tenth Anniversary June 25, 1886, &*

the Fiftieth Anniversary June 25, 1926. El Segundo, Calif.: Upton and Sons, 2006.

Utley, Robert M. *Custer and the Great Controversy*. Los Angeles: Westernlore, 1962.

———. *Frontier Regulars. The United States Army and the Indian, 1866–1890*. New York: Macmillan, 1973.

Utley, Robert M., and Wilcomb E. Washburn. *Indian Wars*. Boston: Houghton Mifflin, 1977.

Van Buren, W. H., M.D., and C. E. Isaccs, M.D. *Illustrated Manual of Operative Surgery and Surgical Anatomy*. New York: Ballière Brothers, 1864.

Walker, L. G., M.D. *Dr. Henry R. Porter: The Surgeon Who Survived Little Bighorn*. Jefferson, N.C.: McFarland, 2008.

Webb, George W. *Chronological List of Engagements between the Regular Army of the United States and Various Tribes of Hostile Indians which Occurred during the Years 1790 to 1898, Inclusive*. New York: AMS, 1976.

Willert, James. *Little Big Horn Diary: A Chronicle of the 1876 Indian War*. El Segundo, Calif.: Upton and Sons, 1997.

———. *March of the Columns. A Chronicle of the 1876 Indian War, June 27–September 16*. El Segundo, Calif.: Upton and Sons, 1994.

Williams, Roger L. *Military Register of Custer's Last Command*. Norman, Okla.: Arthur H. Clark, 2009.

Windolph, Charles. *I Fought with Custer: The Story of Sergeant Windolph, Last Survivor of the Battle of the Little Big Horn, with Explanatory Material and Contemporary Sidelights on the Custer Fight, as Told to Frazier and Robert Hunt*. Lincoln: University of Nebraska Press, 1987.

Wooster, Robert. *The Military and United States Indian Policy, 1865–1903*. New Haven, Conn.: Yale University Press, 1988.

———, ed. *Soldier, Surgeon, Scholar. The Memoirs of William Henry Corbusier, 1844–1930*. Norman: University of Oklahoma Press, 2003.

Articles

Ackernecht, Erwin H. "Anticontagionism between 1821 and 1876." *Bulletin of the History of Medicine* 22 (1948): 562–93.

Ames, Azel. "The Acting Assistant Surgeon of the Army of the United States." *Journal of the Association of Military Surgeons of the United States* 3 (1903): 121–33.

Athearn, Robert G. "The Army and the Plains Indians." *Montana The Magazine of Western History* 6 (1956): 11–22.

———. "The Firewagon Road." *Montana The Magazine of Western History* 20 (1970): 2–19.

Barnard, Frederick A. P. "The Germ Theory of Disease and Its Relations to Hygiene." In *Medical America in the Nineteenth Century,* edited by Gert H. Brieger, 278–92. Baltimore: The Johns Hopkins Press, 1972.

Bill, J. H., M.D. "Notes on Arrow Wounds." *American Journal of Medical Sciences* 44 (1862): 365–87.

Brieger, Gert H. "American Surgery and the Germ Theory of Disease." *Bulletin of the History of Medicine* 40 (1966): 135–45.

Buecker, Thomas R., ed. "A Surgeon at the Little Big Horn: The Letters of Dr. Holmes O. Paulding." *Montana The Magazine of Western History* 32 (Autumn 1982): 34–49.

Clary, David K. "The Role of the Army Surgeon in the West: Daniel Weisel at Fort Davis, Texas, 1868–1872." *Western Historical Quarterly* 3 (1972): 53–66.

Courtwright, David. "Opiate Addiction in the American West, 1850–1920." *Journal of the West* 21 (1982): 23–30.

Cox, John E. "Soldiering in Dakota Territory in the Seventies: A Communication." *North Dakota Historical Quarterly* 6 (1931): 63–81.

Davis, Karen L., and E. Elden Davis, eds. *1876 Big Horn–Yellowstone Journal.* Vols. 1–3 (1993–94).

Dobak, William A. "Yellow-leg Journalists: Enlisted Men as Newspaper Reporters in the Sioux Campaign, 1876." *Journal of the West* 13 (1974): 86–112.

Duffy, John. "Medicine in the West: An Historical Overview." *Journal of the West* 3 (1982): 5–14.

Fox, Richard A., Jr. "West River History: The Indian Village on the Little Bighorn River, June 25–26, 1876." In *Legacy: New Perspectives on the Battle of the Little Bighorn,* edited by Charles E. Rankin, 139–66. Helena: Montana Historical Society Press, 1996.

Gibbon, John. "Hunting Sitting Bull." *American Catholic Quarterly Review* 2 (1877): 665–94. Facsimile copy in *Gibbon on the Sioux Campaign of 1876,* 1–34. Bellevue, NE: Old Army Press, 1969.

———. "Last Summer's Expedition against the Sioux and its Great Catastrophe." *American Catholic Quarterly Review* 2 (1877): 271–304. Facsimile copy in *Gibbon on the Sioux Campaign of 1876,* 35–64. Bellevue, NE: Old Army Press, 1969.

Gillett, Mary C. "United States Army Surgeons and the Big Horn–Yellowstone Expedition of 1876." *Montana The Magazine of Western History* 39 (1989): 16–27.

Godfrey, E. S. "Custer's Last Battle." *Century Magazine* 21 (1891–92): 358–84.

Goldin, Theo W. "On the Little Big Horn with General Custer." *Custer in Periodicals: A Bibliographic Checklist,* edited by John M. Carroll, 98–118. Fort Collins, Colo.: Old Army Press, 1975.

Gray, John S., ed. "Captain Clifford's Newspaper Dispatches." Chicago Westerners *Brand Book* 27 (January 1971): 81–88.

———, ed. "Captain Clifford's Story of the Sioux War of 1876." Chicago Westerners *Brand Book* 26 (December 1969): 73–88.

———, ed. "Captain Clifford's Story—Part II." Chicago Westerners *Brand Book* 26 (January 1970): 81–88.

———. "Medical Service of the Little Big Horn Campaign." Chicago Westerners *Brand Book* 24 (1968): 81–88.

Gressley, Gene M., ed. "A Soldier with Crook: The Letters of H. R. Porter." *Montana The Magazine of Western History* 8 (1958): 33–47.

Hammer, Kenneth M. "Frontier Doctor." Westerners New York Posse *Brand Book* 7 (1960): 55–58.

Hedren, Paul L. "The Sioux War Adventures of Dr. Charles V. Petteys, Acting Assistant Surgeon." *Journal of the West* 32 (April 1993): 29–37.

"Henry R. Porter." In *Compendium of History and Biography of North Dakota.* Chicago: George A. Ogle, 1900.

Kramer, Howard D. "The Germ Theory and the Early Public Health Program in the United States." *Bulletin of the History of Medicine* 22 (1948): 233–47.

Lane, Harrison. "Custer's Massacre: How the News First Reached the Outer World." *Montana The Magazine of Western History* 3 (1952): 46–53.

Lass, William E. "Steamboats on the Yellowstone." *Montana The Magazine of Western History* 35 (1985): 26–41.

Leake, Chauncey D. "The Historical Development of Surgical Anesthesia." *Scientific Monthly* 20 (1925): 304–328.

Lounsberry, Clement. "Dr. H. R. Porter. Thrilling Incidents in the Life of a Bismarck Physician. A Remarkable Steamboat Ride." Reprinted in *Plains Talk* 3 (1972): 2–6.

Luce, Edward S., ed. "The Diaries and Letters of James M. DeWolf." *North Dakota History* 25 (1958): 33–81.

Mardock, Robert W. "Strange Concepts of the American Indian since the Civil War." *Montana The Magazine of Western History* 7 (1957): 36–47.

Mays, B., M.D.; A. Parfitt, M.B.B.S.; and M. J. Hershman, F.R.C.S. "Treatment of Arrow Wounds by Nineteenth Century USA Army Surgeons." *Journal of the Royal Society of Medicine* 87 (1994): 102–103.

McGreevy, Patrick S., M.D., F.A.C.S. "Surgeons at the Little Big Horn." *Surgery, Gynecology & Obstetrics* 140 (1975): 774–80.

McMahon, David E., M.D., and Gregory W. Rutecki, M.D. "In Anticipation of the Germ Theory of Disease: Middleton Goldsmith and the History of Bromine." *Pharos* 74 (Spring 2011): 5–12.

Michno, Greg. "Space Warp: The Effects of Combat Stress at the Little Big Horn." *Journal of the Little Big Horn Associates* 8 (1994): 22–30.

Moffett, W. P. "Henry R. Porter, M.D." Chicago Westerners *Brand Book* 1 (1944–45): 7–10.

Nichols, Ronald H. "Cavalry Firepower: Springfield Carbine's Selection and Performance." *Greasy Grass* 15 (1999): 17–22.

Noyes, Lee C. "Custer's Surgeon, George Lord, among the Missing at the Little Bighorn Battle." *Greasy Grass* 16 (2000): 13–20.

Olch, Peter D. "Medicine in the Indian-Fighting Army, 1866–1890." *Journal of the West* 21 (1982): 32–41.

Petersen, Dr. Edward S. "Surgeons of the Little Big Horn." Chicago West-erners *Brand Book* 3 (1973): 41–43.

Rector, William G. "Fields of Fire. The Reno-Benteen Defense Perimeter." *Montana The Magazine of Western History* 16 (1966): 65–72.

Saum, Lewis O. "Private John F. Donohue's Reflections on the Little Big-horn." *Montana The Magazine of Western History* 50 (2000): 40–53.

Schoenberger, Dale T. "Custer's Scouts." *Montana The Magazine of Western History* 16 (1966): 40–47.

——, ed. "A Trooper with Custer: Augustus DeVoto's Account of the Little Big Horn." *Montana The Magazine of Western History* 40 (1990): 68–71.

Scott, Douglas D. "'An Agreeable Sort When Sober': The Myth of Michael Madden." *Greasy Grass* 25 (May 2009): 24–36.

Sigerist, Henry E., M.D. "Surgery at the Time of the Introduction of Antisepsis." *Journal of the Missouri State Medical Association* 32 (1935): 169–76.

Sklenar, Larry. "Medals for Custer's Men." *Montana The Magazine of Western History* 50 (2000): 54–65.

Stewart, Edgar I. "Little Big Horn 90 Years Later." *Montana The Magazine of Western History* 16 (1966): 2–13.

Walker, L. G., Jr., M.D., F.A.C.S. "Military Medicine at the Little Bighorn." *Journal of the American College of Surgeons* 202 (2006): 191–96.

Wengert, James W. "The Contract Surgeon." *Journal of the West* 36 (1997): 67–76.

Wier, James A. "Nineteenth Century Army Doctors on the Frontier and in Nebraska." *Nebraska History* 61 (1980): 192–214.

Wilson, David A. "Marker Dedicated at Grave of Little Bighorn Survivor." *Battlefield Dispatch* 30 (Winter 2011): 8.

Acknowledgments

I AM GRATEFUL TO T. Juliette Arai in Old Military and Civil Records at the National Archives for providing me with access to the H. R. Porter Papers housed there. The Lane Medical Library at Stanford supplied a trove of nineteenth-century medical and surgical texts, inherited from the early days after it was founded in 1882 as the Cooper Medical College in San Francisco. Independent researcher Elden Davis shared his collection of newspaper articles about Henry Porter, dating from 1872, the year of the physician's first army assignment in Arizona Territory, and continuing up to his death in 1903. Elden was an invaluable correspondent, fielding my many questions with patience and thoughtfulness.

It is my pleasure to thank my agent, Don Lamm, for his unwavering enthusiasm for this story and his fine advice on all manner of detail. I am grateful as well to his colleague at Fletcher & Company Melissa Chinchillo for finding the ideal publishing home for the manuscript. Bert Patenaude suggested ways in which to tell an original and compelling account of this well-known battle. Our countless hours of discussion remain among the high points of this entire project. Researcher and author Paul L. Hedren held the story to the highest standards of historical scholarship, and his suggestions exacted accuracy and authenticity in detail, lexicon, and vernacular. I am in awe of his impressive fluency in all things western.

Publisher Robert A. Clark saw the merit in Porter's story and its window onto the medical dimension of the Battle of the Little Big Horn. Thanks to his vote of confidence this story is now seeing the light of day. Alice Stanton, my editor at the University of Oklahoma Press, was a genial and efficient impresario who facilitated and coordinated all the innumerable elements involved in turning an unpolished book manuscript into a reader-ready book. Editor Kevin Brock masterfully tamed my writing into lean and crisp prose.

Charlotte Stevenson and Lisa Joo provided invaluable technical assistance. Finally, my husband, David, always a voice of encouragement, endured many a hike in Death Valley, where as a form of field research, I attempted to approximate the inhospitable conditions experienced by the men in the hilltop fight.

Index